ETHICAL LEADERSHIP
THROUGH
TRANSFORMING JUSTICE

Thomas F. McMahon

University Press of America,® Inc.
Dallas · Lanham · Boulder · New York · Oxford

I dedicate this book to Patricia Werhane and Mary Ann McGrath — two women who served as muses, devil's advocates and catalysts in the production and publication of this book.

TABLE OF CONTENTS

FORWARD

"The just man justices": so writes Jesuit poet Gerard Manley Hopkins. And the just scholar writes about justice. At least he does if he is Father Thomas McMahon, one of the few humans to have earned a doctorate in theology and an M.B.A. Tom and I did a research project in business ethics together 35 years ago, and I have admired his research and teaching ever since. The research included a project on the teaching of ethics in collegiate schools of business. The teaching included weekend seminars for students of Loyola University Chicago, always focusing on socio-ethical values in business. The topics included: acquisitions and mergers; affirmative action and reverse discrimination; plant closings; etc. The virtue of justice was regularly central to these sessions. So I was not surprised to learn that this book is fundamentally theoretical, but also has case studies of eight good human beings who exemplified the just behavior that Tom is describing. He is scholarly, but he values ethical conduct very highly. This is evident from his definition of transforming justice: rights combined with power effects justice.

Scholars, teachers and graduate students engaged in the social sciences, business and moral theology will be challenged and intrigued by this book. Administrators who practice transforming justice in their decision-making will lead their organizations in socially admirable ways.

Raymond Baumhart, S.J.
November, 2003

PREFACE

Several readers of this manuscript have asked me why I chose these particular eight leaders to illustrate the concept of Transforming Justice. There were a number of reasons for this choice. In a broad sense, I wanted diversity in professions and careers, gender, religion, basic philosophy and commitment to a specific goal or an objective. The purpose for these various perspectives was to illustrate that Transforming Justice is applicable in situations that include diverse ways of life. Transforming Justice is not limited to one specific point of view. Its application includes many kinds of variations.

Another reason for selecting these eight Profiled Leaders is that each ultimately sharpened his or her focus to a specific cause that had a social dimension. A sharp focus is one of the conditions for Transforming Justice. In addition to a sharp focus, all eight people employed essentially nonviolent means to attain their goals, although nonviolence is not necessarily a prescribed condition for Transforming Justice. Since September 11, 2001 the concept of violence itself has been transformed for most people, especially for Americans. Some support all-out war by any method against all terrorists. Others believe that peace can only be achieved when all people are treated equally as human beings and share in the goods of the earth. All those Profiled Leaders received or developed sufficient power to bring about important changes in a specific segment of society. The use of this power efficiently and effectively is the underpinning rationale for Transforming Justice. Simultaneously and in an illustrative manner, all had rights that were essentially different. Such rights, especially human rights, are the material of justice. Power is frequently needed to exercise these rights in order to bring about justice. But the use of power in each case was consistent with the justice they desired to, and ultimately did, achieve.

The importance of the people chosen for discussion in this book has been corroborated by several sources. A distinguished panel of twenty contributors, including television anchorman Dan Rather and former New York governor Mario Cuomo, was formed to determine a list of people who had the greatest impact on the twentieth century. The people the panel selected had either a positive (e.g., Pope John Paul II) or a negative impact on society (e.g., Stalin). The panel chose three leaders of the eight of those profiled in this book, namely Mahatma Gandhi, Martin Luther King, Jr. and Nelson Mandela. A *Time Magazine* open poll on leaders and revolutionaries included Nelson Mandela (#2) and Martin Luther King, Jr. (#9). This panel mentioned earlier also included Pope John Paul II and Lech Walesa in their list, while the *Time* poll named Mother Teresa (#5). This latter group without a doubt are important contributors to society, but their focus was too broad to clearly illustrate Transforming Justice. (Recall that Walesa went from the overturn of the communist regime in Poland into politics and subsequently engaged in an unsuccessful presidency that allegedly included corruption.) Both John Paul II and Mother Teresa have had a worldwide impact on society, but in a sense too broad a scope for the specific focus that Transforming Justice requires.

It is important to emphasize that the description of those profiled in the beginning of the book and their relevance to Transforming Justice is incorporated into the exposition of the components of Transforming Justice, namely rights, power and justice. The components are not treated as distinct entities from the leaders profiled. It might even be said that the components subsume and provide structure to the specific but diverse activities of these Profiled Leaders. Towards the end of the book the similarities and differences among those profiled are compared to illustrate various forms of Transforming Justice in terms of rights, power and justice. Thus, the exposition of Transforming Justice should be seen as a single unit, although there is the method of exposition changes from the inductive approach of the Profiled to the deductive approach of the components of Transforming Justice, and finally to an amalgamation of both in the Observations and Conclusions of this book.

ACKNOWLEDGMENTS

Many individuals whom I respect and to whom I am grateful encouraged the creation and production of this book in a number of different ways. I thank them all and keep them in my thoughts and prayers.

The Clerics of St. Viator have been my second family since I joined the order in 1946. My affiliation with this group nurtured my desire to teach and encouraged my intellectual pursuit of the field of Business Ethics. In particular Fr. Charles G. Bolser, C.S.V., Provincial, Clerics of St. Viator of the United States Provinces, Fr. Robert E. Erickson, C.S.V., and Brother Leo V. Ryan, C.S.V., were instrumental in moving this project forward. In addition, I am grateful to the former Provincial, Fr. Robert M. Egan, who encouraged me from the outset of this project. The genesis of this book was a presentation at the Annual Meeting of the Society for Business Ethics (SBE) in August of 1986. Br. Leo Ryan and Pat Werhane, who at that time were President and Executive Secretary of the Society, invited me to deliver a talk at a plenary session. I chose as the topic for this talk to explicate the concept of Transforming Justice for the first time. Previous to the speech, I was fortunate to have several talented colleagues read drafts of the original talk. Robert Erickson, C.S.V. (colleague and mathematician), James Fanale, C.S.V. (a former student of mine with a Ph.D. in English), and Loyola Chicago Professors Michael Keeley (Management), Walter Krowlakowski. S.J. (Education), and Ruth McGugan (English) reviewed and reacted related to their respective specialties. Their lively comments and the reactions of the scholars at this SBE gathering prompted me to move forward and clarify the construct of Transforming Justice, first through the publication of an article in the *Business Ethics Quarterly* and secondly with this larger book project.

The School of Business Administration at Loyola University Chicago provided me with a home to teach and write for 28 years. It was the seminal work and winning personality of former Loyola University President Raymond Baumhart,

S.J. that attracted me to the university and sparked my interest in this academic area. Two premier Business Ethicists at Loyola, Professors Al Gini and John Boatright have helped clarify my thinking and offered excellent insights into the process of producing this book. I remain grateful for the friendship and intellectual stimulation provided by Professors John O'Malley, Ronald Rudolph, and John Jozwiak, our original Socio-Legal Studies Department. I am grateful for the support and encouragement of School of Business Dean Robert Parkinson, a former MBA student of mine, and to colleagues in the School of Business: Professors Sue Vondran, Raymond Benton and Mary Ann McGrath. I am especially indebted to Kathleen King, who tirelessly typed, formatted, proofread, reformatted and provided me with her expertise, good cheer and an abundance of candy to keep the project moving forward.

Last, but surely not least, I want to thank my family for their continuous support of my vocation as a priest and teacher. In our lively Irish-German family we have always joked that everyone talks and no one listens. It was my parents, brothers and sisters who served as my first teachers in the concepts of faith, rights, justice and power. We have all grown into adulthood with strong positive values. We really were listening to each other after all.

Thomas F. McMahon, C.S.V.

November, 2003

INTRODUCTION

The development of the concept of Transforming Justice is an attempt to view justice as a realistic concept that reflects an operating down-to-earth reality. More often than not, justice is presented as a theory to render what is due to a person or to establish equality between individuals. Justice, however, is more than theory. It is the practical application of respecting the rights of others. Justice *does something*. Transforming Justice, as a specific form of justice as discussed in this book, does something quite important. It interrelates the rights and the power of individuals into the concept of justice. In fact, it actually *integrates* rights, power and justice. This is a dramatic change from the traditional and contemporary treatises on justice.

I first introduced the concept of Transforming Justice in a basic form to the Society for Business Ethics at its annual meeting in 1993. It was well received, but dramatic changes in its explication as well as some examples for its visualization were necessary. A short version of Transforming Justice appeared in the *Encyclopedic Dictionary of Business Ethics* in 1996. A more developed presentation was published in the October 1999 issue of *Business Ethics Quarterly*. These two publications provided a birds-eye view of this innovative and captivating concept of justice. In this monograph, I undertake the task of presenting Transforming Justice as a viable, indeed necessary, perspective to the traditional understanding of justice. This book not only reviews justice in its many perceptions, but also it goes a step further by illustrating Transforming Justice in the eight Profiles of twentieth century leaders in social causes. The reader is probably familiar with these Profiled Leaders from history, news reports and other media coverage. But to date, these important leaders have not been connected to the concept of Transforming Justice. That is what this book does. It demonstrates how these Profiled Leaders integrated rights, power and justice in order to change a segment of society. This process is what I refer to as *Transforming Justice*.

This book will examine Transforming Justice from several different perspectives and will adhere to the following format. First the topic will be introduced and a working definition of Transforming Justice will be proposed in Chapter 1. In Chapter 2, profiles of eight selected people who have exercised Transforming Justice in the Twentieth Century will be examined. Chapter 3 is an in-depth presentation of its components of the model, namely, rights, power and justice. Some readers might not feel the necessity of reviewing this theoretical aspect of Transforming Justice. The practical application of these components will be covered in the Observation section of Chapter 4. Also in Chapter 4, a formal definition of Transforming Justice is proposed along with a visualization of the concept utilizing a Venn diagram. In addition, observations and conclusions are presented for further discussion.

CHAPTER 1

What is Transforming Justice?

Chapter 1 will include four aspects of Transforming Justice. The first Section A. *Transforming Justice: In the Beginning,* describes the occasion for the development of the concept. Section B. *The Development of a Concept,* shows the inter-relatedness of rights, power and justice. Section C. *How to Describe the Concept,* examines the two basic notions of "justice" and "transforming." Section D. *Nominal Definition,* presents a working or operational definition of Transforming Justice. A formal definition of Transforming Justice is proposed in Chapter 4 of this book.

A. *Transforming Justice: In the Beginning*

The year was 1968. It was a time of political and ideological turmoil. The United States was in a state of reevaluating its role in the Vietnam War. The war and various social issues became the material for panel discussions, television talk shows, interview programs and discussions around dining room tables and water coolers. Basic assumptions about institutions were being questioned and challenged. There was a concern for the rights of minorities in public schools, in private clubs and in corporate businesses and institutions, both religious and secular. Simultaneously, it was a time of turmoil within the Catholic Church. Vatican II opened many "windows" for the faithful—the laity, the religious and the priests. It also opened the windows to non-Roman Catholics throughout the world. These "windows" blew in fresh ideas to mix with the assumptions of an aging, hierarchical institution.

In my small world of seminary teaching, many students and some of the priest teachers, made the serious and sometimes painful decision to leave the sheltered life of the seminary in order to assume roles as lay people in what was thought to be a more "real" and larger society. Seminary enrollments dropped dramatically. Many administrators and faculty of Catholic religious orders in Washington, D.C., realized that it would be impossible to keep their seminaries open with so few faculty and students.   They decided to consolidate the resources of their seminarians and their teachers; in so doing they developed a new concept and structure in Catholic seminaries for the teaching of religious brothers and priests. Instead of individual houses of learning, they formed the Washington Theological Coalition. The first step in this process was to have professors teach in seminaries other than their own to test how effective this proposed union would be. As Professor of Moral Theology at the Viatorian Seminary, I was asked to teach Josephite seminarians on their own campus. The Josephite religious community is generally recognized for its missionary work in the rural southeastern United States. The seminarians were mostly African-American. Part of their pastoral ministry as seminarians in Washington was directed to working with the city's large African-American community. In the course of our time together I taught them about rights and justice and illustrated the concepts with many applications. We also discussed the social responsibility of institutions, both non-profit and for-profit.   These included business corporations and private institutions, including the religious communities to which we all belonged.

The students were enthusiastically receptive until the night when the Reverend Martin Luther King, Jr. was assassinated. At that point, Washington turned violent in a way not heretofore witnessed in the United States. The city was in flames in the 7th, 14th and H Street corridors. Riots broke out. It appeared that chaos reigned and mob violence predominated the black neighborhoods. After my class, aptly entitled "Justice", the seminarians would go to these areas to try to minister to the many African-American victims. Emotionally shaken and bewildered by what they had seen day after day during the riots, the seminarians would come to class and ask: "Where are the rights of these people? Where is the justice you talk about in class?" With good reason, they challenged me in each class during the semester. They pleaded for answers to their plaintiff cries for justice.

These seminarians were trying to reconcile classroom theory with their daily ministry. Through their questions, they forced me to re-examine my own view of rights and justice. It gradually became clear to me that the possession of human and civil rights in and of themselves does not necessarily require others to respect them. There was more to the practice of justice than the current theory was providing. Something was missing.

Upon reflection, it dawned on me that the missing ingredient for effective justice was *power.* In the traditional presentation of the tract in moral theology termed *de justitia*, rights, power and justice were treated more often as separate and parallel entities, rather than as interacting and inter-related components of the same concept, namely, justice. It became clear to me that unless persons have some degree of power, they cannot either demand that their rights be respected or are able to respect the rights of others. It takes power to make certain that rights are respected. The fundamental theme of Transforming Justice is that justice cannot, and therefore will not, become an existential reality unless its theory also includes the notion of power. Power is what the Josephite seminarians needed to experience in their search for justice in the riot-ridden corridors of Washington, D.C. Power is what makes justice "transforming." Power has the capacity to move away from inequality in fact (and not in theory only) to equality as a reality (and not in theory only). Transforming Justice is more than an approach, a frame of reference, or a description. It is an existential reality.

B. *The Development of a Concept*

The notion of justice as an *active* virtue goes beyond a simple, static determination of what is "just". It touches the realities of life that everyone experiences daily. In these everyday experiences of life, rights and power appear not to be separated. Upon reflection, the separation of rights from power both in theory and in action is analogous to the separation of the "sensory" from the "imaginative" in art and in life. (Jaffe, 1964.) Imagination is the formation of a mental image of something never before perceived in reality. Sensory pertains to something that is grasped, comprehended or known. The need to devise a framework of justice that brings out the wholeness of its existential being is the underlying rationale for developing the theory of Transforming Justice. The *concept* of Transforming Justice is "imaginative." The *existence* of Transforming Justice is "sensory" insofar as it is recognized as a vibrant reality.

Another purpose for developing this theory is to suggest a conceptual framework for ethics that incorporates both rights and power into the notion of values and justice. Ethicists frequently approach these issues in terms of value, rights and justice; power has no place in this framework. Others view social action only in terms of power; apart from legitimate claims, rights, especially human rights, become inconsequential. Thus, it is necessary for a conceptual framework of justice to incorporate both the dynamics of power and the qualifying aspects of rights.

C. *How to Describe the Concept*

As a theory, Transforming Justice is a systematically organized body of knowledge whereby rights, power, and justice interact. It also contains assumptions and rules for analyzing this interaction. It is a position or stand that leads to an application; it is an operative justice. While abstract in itself, the theory of Transforming Justice is geared towards activity. It is not static; it is thoroughly dynamic. The interaction between rights and power in Transforming Justice challenges the traditional view that rights and power are parallel factors in human behavior, as stated previously. The traditional approach to justice treats rights and power as two separate entities, akin to apples and oranges. To the contrary, Transforming Justice postulates an "action-reaction" relationship between rights and power.

Rarely are rights traditionally associated with power. For example, business managers may complain that a forthcoming boycott of their products is "blackmail." They may view such a boycott as an abuse of power. But from the opposite side of the transaction the persons who threaten the boycott may claim that the purchase or non-purchase of particular brands at certain stores is simply an exercise of their rights in a free market contract. (The forthcoming Profiles illustrate the power of boycotts in certain situations in both public and private sectors.) Similarly, it is rarely stated that a judge in a court of law in awarding a claim to a plaintiff is exercising abusive power: both plaintiff and defendant have legitimate claims or rights. One party more certain, greater and clearer claims than the other. The judge or the jury has the power to evaluate these claims. Both plaintiff and defendant possess claims that have to be evaluated. When the judge or jury comes to a decision, either the plaintiff or the defendant will be given some vindication and/or award. The party who receives a positive judgment often declares: "justice has been done." The loser, on the contrary, might seek an appeal, which is an operational method of asserting that "my rights were not respected, and that justice had not been granted." Thus, it is in the practical order—not necessarily in abstractions—where rights and power interact. This is the milieu for Transforming Justice.

The following paragraphs will detail the two pivotal terms in the title, "justice" and "transforming", as they apply towards an understanding of Transforming Justice. "Justice," a substantive, or noun, will be briefly treated here but will be thoroughly discussed in Chapter 3 as a component of Transforming Justice. However, "transforming", a participial adjective, will be treated in this section.

Justice

Justice is defined basically as rendering to a person what is due to that person. Justice is treated in this book primarily, but not exclusively, as a moral virtue: that is, the *constant* and *perpetual* will to render to each person what is due. Ulpian, a jurist during the Roman Empire, defined justice in a manner that is still used by many ethicists and legal scholars as an appropriate definition. In this early sense, justice is a *habit* that constantly and perpetually seeks equality among persons. Justice, as a moral virtue, deals with the *means* to its end. Many scholars, like Thomas Aquinas, consider the end to be equality. Rawls (1971) and others view the end or purpose of justice to bring about fairness. Thus, justice, the moral virtue, is concerned with the means to achieve equality and fairness. It does not of itself treat the end or the goal of justice. It attempts to answer the question: "What actions will lead to equality?"

Transforming Justice is also about efficient and effective means to attain equality. (The notion of equality will be treated extensively in Chapter 3.)

Transforming Justice is operative (that is, it gets things done) and normative (it has standards that must be met). This equality can be measured in a one-to-one exchange, as in a buyer-seller contract that can be as simple as buying a shirt at Macy's. This is arithmetic equality: one buys and another sells at an agreed upon price. Equality can also be proportional, as one person pays taxes and thereby contributes the common good (one-to-many) or the common good is shared with an individual in need through the welfare system (many-to-one).

However, Transforming Justice is not merely descriptive, such as the end-result of a survey or census. It is normative; it sets standards for equality. Simultaneously, Transforming Justice is not a type of critical justice, the type employed by ecologists when they challenge the federal government for permitting private companies to purchase public lands for paper mills or for petroleum extraction.

Transforming

The concept of transformation is often inductively learned. Like many boys in grade school, I had a model electric train. It was a small-scale copy of the Baltimore and Ohio's "Royal Blue". The train used direct current reduced in voltage. The transformer, which changed the alternating current of the Commonwealth Edison Company to direct current required by the model train, was an integral component for operating the train. It provided the electricity for the train to circle the track. Power from the transformer became the source of the train's movement. Electric power transformed the train from a motionless mixture of metals to a moving vehicle that scared our dog. It also burned to a crisp the tin-foil icicles that fell from the Christmas tree. An electric transformer changes the amount and kind of electricity; it does not change its "substance." It remains electric power. Power is also a necessity for Transforming Justice to achieve equality, not only in individuals but also in the broad-spectrum of society.

In the practical order of things, what does "transforming" mean? Etymologists generally state that the infinitive "to transform" means to "change shape," or even to change the "function" of a particular being (*The American Heritage Dictionary*, 1976). Adding the suffix "-ing" to the word "transform" makes it a participial adjective that affects the notion of "justice." It suggests some form of change in justice. Adding "transforming" does not in itself change the definition of justice as "rendering what is due to a person." It seems that "transforming" could also apply to social change. In some way, many pivotal people in history, such as Martin Luther, "transformed" the society with which they interacted. Similarly, the eight leaders of the twentieth century profiled in Chapter 2 of this book brought about change in their specific segments of society.

Transforming Justice might also reflect the notion of "change" in the sciences of mathematics and physics. In mathematics, "transforming" is a change in form without alteration of quantity or value. In physics, "transforming" may be a change of energy from one form (alternating current) to another (direct current), as exemplified above. Thus, it can be seen in the physical sciences that "transformation" does not necessarily require a change of substance (electricity) but rather a change in the type of providing electricity (direct or alternating current) and in mathematics no change in quantity and value.   It is important to emphasize again that the "transforming" in Transforming Justice does not affect the substance of justice, "to render to each person that which is due." It only affects the *means* whereby justice is achieved. Later in Chapter 2, the series of Profiles of pivotal historical figures of the twentieth century will illustrate the means that most of these transformers utilized to bring about Transforming Justice—boycotts, marches, fasting, non-cooperation with the government regulations—all within the context of nonviolence and civil disobedience.   Hopefully, there will be similar transformers in the twenty-first century and beyond.   Unfortunately, terrorists have negatively transformed society in the early twenty-first century.   Their violent activities in no way reflect or parallel the Transforming Justice of the Profiled Leaders of the twentieth century.

"Transforming" might also suggest a process or a progression in change.   Transforming Justice allows a continuum, which includes a "lesser" or "greater" dimension.   This statement could be challenged because the moral virtue of justice is concerned only with what is owed.   Justice can be thought of as in a dichotomous sense of being either present or absent; that is, there is no more or less.   Aristotle and Aquinas wrote that only justice has an objective norm called the *medium rei* (the real mean), which does not allow for the greater or lesser dimension of a continuum.   The *medium rei* does not respect the subjective or contextual condition of the giver (lender) or the receiver (borrower). It respects only the fact.   For example, if a poor person owes a wealthy person fifty dollars, his poverty does not affect the obligation to pay back the exact amount borrowed.   The traditional definition—rendering to each his or her due—refers to what is owed and not to the financial condition of the borrower or the lender. If the lender forgives the fifty-dollar debt, he or she does not exercise justice; the lender in this situation may be performing an act of liberality.   Religious idealism might insist that this kind of debt be canceled or forgiven.   Transforming Justice in no way relegates charity to a lower form of moral contribution to society.   It rather perceives charity as an underpinning of justice.   The other cardinal virtues of fortitude, temperance and prudence incorporate the subjective aspect of the person.   For example, the amount of alcohol in the blood of an automobile driver determines if he/she is legally intoxicated.   A legally intoxicated person frequently violates the cardinal virtue of temperance, however, this latter violation may depend upon the metabolism of the individual.

While justice of itself does not allow a relative or contextual continuum, "transforming" is a process that allows for such variability.

Transforming Justice may be experienced in its varying stages similar to the gradual intellectual development of a child through the educational process. The Profiled Leaders in Chapter 2 illustrate these changes, especially in the cases of Susan B. Anthony, Mahatma Gandhi, Martin Luther King, Jr. and Nelson Mandela. These historical figures had to search, sometimes through trial and error, to find efficient and effective means towards their goal of justice.

Up to this point, "transforming" in its most accepted definition, means to "change shape." How is the shape of justice changed in the case of Transforming Justice? This question will be treated at length and fully developed in the section on justice. At this point, a simple explanation may be illustrative. Justice becomes transformed into Transforming Justice when power becomes intrinsic to the concept. For example, after African-Americans were granted "equal protection under the law" through the Fourteenth Amendment to the U.S. Constitution, the U.S. Supreme Court in 1890 ruled that "separate but equal protection" fulfilled this obligation. This decision in effect approved segregation in public places, facilities and schools. This decision was effective until 1954 when the U.S. Supreme Court under Chief Justice Earl Warren ruled in the *Brown v. the School Board of Topeka, Kansas* (374 U.S. 483 [1954]) that segregation was unconstitutional. Segregation was deemed unlawful, but the decision as such did not require *integration* of the races.

The Civil Rights Act of 1964 prohibited racial and sexual discrimination in the workplace. The Equal Employment Occupational Commission provided a resource to obtain power. Employees who charged their employer with racial or sexual discrimination were given legal means to exercise their newly obtained rights. Overburdened with cases (some without merit) and insufficient resources created a significant bottleneck towards eliminating discrimination. The process was slow and employees frequently felt powerless. Thus, rights without power are merely nominal. Another source of power can be group action. Saul Alinsky realized this early in his career as a social activist in Chicago. Unions acknowledge the role of power by increasing the number of members. Other groups, such as the American Association of Retired Persons, select specific areas like Medicare as the focus for the exertion of their substantial aggregate power.

Relations are natural and logical associations between two or more beings or entities. Power and justice are both relational; they are thus other-directed, whereby they are apart but interact with each other. The same can be said of rights. Rights can interact with justice and become the material of justice. In fact, rights precede justice. (Pieper, 1965) Like power and justice, rights are relational and other-directed. Rights, power and justice are all relational and, indeed, inter-relational. As such these constructs have the capacity to affect each other. In particular, power becomes the primary agent for change in justice, while it does not destroy its substance. Intimate and interacting relations can sometimes produce a new "being" or entity. The interaction of rights, power and justice has produced a new entity termed

Transforming Justice. This interaction and interrelationship is discussed further and visualized in the Venn Diagram of Chapter 4.

This interrelationship may take place within a local, regional, national or international milieu. Additionally, specificity directs Transforming Justice to a particular topic, such as the right of women to vote in public elections. It also stipulates the kind and degree of power, which could be progressively increased over time as described in most of the individual Profiled Leaders. It can also be instantly acquired, as in a monarchy such as accrues to British royalty and the Roman Catholic papacy. Or it may be granted through law, such as in the case of judgeships, where, for example, a person gains more power in advancing from county court into the role of a federal judge. Rights may be human, civil, legal, moral or any combination of these. Equality may be attained through the various species of justice, such as exchange, contributive, distributive, social, compensatory, and procedural or a combination of these. These concepts will be discussed in the section on justice.

D. *Nominal Definition*

The interaction of rights, power and justice in Transforming Justice is defined nominally or operationally in this simple statement: rights plus power equals justice. It is important for this conceptual framework to incorporate the dynamism of power with the qualifying aspects of rights. With power as an integral part of the concept, Transforming Justice can only exist in an operating form. It is that "value-added" dimension of power and rights working together that specifically qualifies humans and their behavior.

As presented in this book, Transforming Justice is viewed within the context of dramatic social changes in the Twentieth Century. It is within this framework, rather than that of the 1968 riots, that the many facets of Transforming Justice evolved in my thinking and my teaching. The questions of the Loyola University Chicago School of Business Administration MBA students were no less challenging than those of the Josephite seminarians in Washington, D.C. The underlying concern is the same: How can justice to be attained as a reality and not just postulated as a necessary "good" for an individual or a group in society? In some respect, Transforming Justice can be "sensed": a person can feel, enjoy, realize, touch, embrace, or experience it. I believe that it was this "sensing" and not the cold abstraction that appealed to my students. However, it is not a "touching-feeling" kind of justice, because it deals with the qualitative aspect of rights and the quantitative dimension of power. Both stand on their own as valid components of Transforming Justice.

Once again, the nominal or working definition of Transforming Justice is simple. Rights combined with power effects justice. The Profiled Leaders clearly illustrate the different ways that Transforming Justice can be attained. They all had rights. They all ultimately achieved enough power to exercise their rights and thus to "transform" a particular segment of society. They all exercised a particular type of Transforming Justice.

CHAPTER 2

Eight Profiled Leaders - Praenotanda

The definition of Transforming Justice is abstract and conceptual. To understand Transforming Justice as it has been applied to the "real world," it is useful to illustrate its various aspects and approaches through actual case studies. In the following pages the lives of eight twentieth-century people whose actions exemplify Transforming Justice are detailed. They have all used power to bring about change for just causes. However, in each case the kind of power, the perception of rights, and the type of transformation differ. Each is a distinct application of Transforming Justice.

These cases are not meant to be biographies. All the lives of the people mentioned subsequently have autobiographies, biographies and extensive media coverage, both written and visual. These are available in libraries and bookstores for further information and in-depth study. The case studies selectively review those aspects of their lives that have contributed to their exercise of Transforming Justice. The cases are presented in chronological order, although some of the time frames overlap. One case is not necessarily more important than another. They are presented as people who have contributed to Transforming Justice in a particular manner.

The first case is Susan B. Anthony's long campaign to obtain federal legislation for women's suffrage. It is followed by Mahatma Gandhi's insistence on nonviolence. Gandhi's nonviolent means not only affected a change in the British Establishment's control in India, but it also influenced Martin Luther King, Jr. and Cesar Chavez in the United States and, to a degree, Nelson Mandela in South Africa. Federal Judge Frank Johnson used the United States Constitution to permit boycotts of a city bus company, to uphold the rights of Freedom Riders to enter Southern segregated cities, and to allow what is now assessed to have been an historic march to Selma. Martin Luther King, Jr. was also instrumental in these three decisions. Pope John XXIII transformed the Roman Catholic Church itself and its relationship to the rest of the world. Cesar Chavez primarily transformed the position of migrant farm workers within the United States. Nelson Mandela effectively showed how patience and persistence can produce a free and democratic nation. Aaron Feuerstein in the Malden Mills case used his economic power to bring about Transforming Justice in a Massachusetts city.

These eight cases exemplify Transforming Justice in ways that are illustrative, though far from exhaustive. Additionally, they all contain the three components of Transforming Justice; namely, rights, power, and justice. These components will be treated separately and more fully later on in this book.

Of the three components, rights are not always clear or certain. A person or a class of persons can have a moral right, but not necessarily a legal or civil right. This issue is covered in the presentation of Susan B. Anthony, Mahatma Gandhi, Martin Luther King, Jr., Cesar Chavez, Nelson Mandela and the employees of the Malden Mills.

The application of power also differs in each example. Sometimes it is manifested as economic power, as in the case Feuerstein and the Malden Mills. In other cases it is in the form of legal power, as exercised by Judge Frank Johnson. Sometimes it is social power, as in the instance of Martin Luther King, Jr. At other times it is political power, as demonstrated by Nelson Mandela. Sometimes it is legislative power, as with Susan B. Anthony. Sometimes it is the power of a unified group, as with the union of Chavez. Occasionally it is papal power, in the case of John XXIII. Each case exemplifies how power is used to effect Transforming Justice.

The justice achieved in Transforming Justice was obtained within a specific social context. For Susan B. Anthony the context involved the lack of the civil rights for women in the United States. Gandhi and Mandela both sought political justice in their respective contexts. Martin Luther King, Jr. and Cesar Chavez sought social justice. With John XXIII, justice relates to the dignity and rights of people, including religious freedom. With respect to Frank Johnson, the context was legal justice. In the case of the Malden Mills the goal was justice toward employees. At the time this exceeded the minimal demands of civil law. As can be seen from the Profiled Leaders, Transforming Justice has many different applications as justice itself does.

None of these people sought Transforming Justice as such. The term was not in their vocabulary. It is said that actions speak louder than words. Each personal example cited is a person who pursued rights, both human and civil, while possessing the power to exercise these rights. By their actions they transformed a segment of society. They attempted to bring about some form of equality and fairness through their transforming action. And an end or objective of justice is equality. Perhaps unknowingly, these selected people—the Profiled Leaders—exercised Transforming Justice.

Transforming Justice favors nonviolence. The studies bear this out. Nonetheless, the nonviolence approach may incidentally occasion physical force, as in the cases of Gandhi, King, Chavez and Mandela. Although each of these men condemned violence, they foresaw that civil disobedience had the power to trigger physical reaction on the part of government agencies. The governments at times used force to counteract acts of civil disobedience. This became obvious in the slaughter of Indians by the British troops. Even the jailing of Susan B. Anthony may be considered a mild form of governmental force.

Nonviolence can also be an exercise of power, primarily when groups are formed to promote a particular objective or to stop an offensive practice. Theoretically, boycotts, marches, sit-ins and other similar forms of protest are nonviolent acts of power. They are performed by groups of individuals who favor or oppose a position of a government, an industry or a company. All of the case studies exemplify the use of nonviolent means of power to obtain Transforming Justice.

SUSAN B. ANTHONY

"I would rather make history than write it."

Susan B. Anthony

Susan B. Anthony was born into a male-dominated society. The U.S. Congress in the late 1800s was not an exception to this patriarchal system. The social activists of the post-Civil War period were more interested in temperance than in the rights of women. Women were expected to follow their traditional role (drawn from the Germans) as *kinder* (producers of children), *kuchen* (cooks for the family) and *kirche* (church-goers). Susan B. Anthony did not accept this traditional role. She was an activist who challenged many of the assumptions of her society. As an example, some activists, including Susan B. Anthony herself, felt that President Lincoln did not go far enough by simply freeing the slaves. They thought that the freed slaves should be protected, either through a presidential executive order or through legislation. Furthermore, women's rights during that period were rarely the prime interest of the abolition social activists. In the political sphere at that time, women were not to be seen or heard. Susan B. Anthony maintained her own focus and vision in this setting: the equality of women in the male-dominated society of her epoch. The political context and agenda made the campaign for women's rights an almost overwhelming challenge. It became the primary, if not only, focus of her life's work. Ultimately, she won, even though she never participated in her victory of a woman's right to vote in a federal election.

Born in 1820 into a strong Quaker family, Susan B. Anthony has always been identified with the woman's suffrage movement. Although she fought for various social reforms throughout her life, including temperance and abolition, she finally focused on obtaining a constitutional amendment for women to vote. She believed that only through legal means, through the addition to the U.S. Constitution of an amendment allowing women to vote, would women be free to pursue their other rights, such as the right to own property, the right to equal pay for equal work, job opportunities equal to those of men and equitable divorce settlements. She also believed that universal justice and equality would follow such a constitutional amendment. (Harper, 1998)

Anthony attempted to get the all-male congress to pass legislation for women's right to vote, but this petition was consistently rejected. At the outset, she was not able to get political party platforms to include the plank of women's suffrage. (Du Boise, 1922) The refusals became less adamant as her attempts gradually produced positive efforts in some states, mostly in the Western region of the United States. Several states allowed women to vote in state elections. However, she died in 1906, before the XIX Amendment that permitted women to vote in national elections became law in 1920. History has demonstrated that women's suffrage alone has not corrected many of the inequalities that exist between women and men in American society. Over the years women's rights were legislated piecemeal to include many of the reforms that Anthony initially proposed. (Harper, 1998) She actively contributed to state suffrage campaigns, especially in the West. But there were no uncomplicated or easy victories. Although women from some of the Western states were enfranchised before women in other areas, each territory and each state had its own issues and obstacles. She found this out in the early victories in Wyoming, Utah, Colorado and Idaho. In New York State she began a campaign in 1854 to expand the 1848 Married Women's Property Law. She was criticized when she campaigned with the racist Democrat George Francis Train in Kansas, where she compromised her fundamental principle of nonviolence. (Harper, 1998) Anthony compromised in order to focus more sharply on her basic concern, suffrage for women. In 1869 she founded the National Woman Suffrage Association (NWSA) with her close ally and friend, Elizabeth Cady Stanton, to pursue her final goal of universal women's suffrage.

Like other social reformers, such as Gandhi, Martin Luther King, Jr., Chavez and Mandela (all reviewed in the following sections of the Profiled Leaders), Anthony employed civil disobedience to pursue her goal. She voted in the 1872 presidential election, and was soon arrested by a U.S. Marshall for having committed the federal crime of casting a vote by a woman. She was subsequently indicted, tried and convicted of voting illegally *(United States v. Susan B. Anthony, 1873)*. Together with Cady Stanton, Anthony wrote and delivered the "Declaration of the Rights of Women" at the Centennial Exposition in Philadelphia. They also wrote the four-volume *History of Woman Suffrage*, as well as other position papers. In terms of proclaiming the rights of women, Anthony and Stanton were inseparable. Unfortunately, the pair both died before the enactment and ratification of the Nineteenth Amendment.   Susan B. Anthony's philosophy and *modus agendi* can best be summarized in her own words: "There can be but one possible way for women to be freed from the degradation of disenfranchisement and this is through the slow process of agitation and education, until the vast majority of women themselves desire freedom." (Harper, 1998, 2:918)

Susan B. Anthony's long and tedious journey for women's suffrage exemplifies Transforming Justice. Although her thesis that women's suffrage would automatically carry with it other women's rights proved to be erroneous, her efforts did ultimately transform civil rights for women in the United States.

Anthony fulfilled the conditions for Transforming Justice. First of all, her focus was for others, specifically women. Secondly, her actions, for the most part, were ethically good means to an ethically good end. Nonviolence was intrinsically embedded in her approach. Thirdly, she sought civil rights to effect actual equality for women. For her, women have natural rights that should be respected. Fourthly, her goal of women's suffrage indeed transformed the role of women in society. She gradually built a power base that ultimately challenged legislators, even those in the U.S. Congress. Subsequent legislation, such as the 1963 Equal Pay Act and the 1964 Civil Rights Act, went further by forbidding sexual discrimination at work. Indeed, Susan B. Anthony exemplified the concept of Transforming Justice in her persistent effort to attain equality between men and women. She sought to fulfill the 1776 *Declaration of Rights* that all are created equal. She followed a legal approach in addition to a moral approach toward the goal of achieving equality. Indeed, she exemplifies *Legal Transforming Justice*. Her power developed gradually over the years of her commitment to women's rights that were, in the end, accepted by women and men in the United States. And, finally, her moral imagination expanded her vision and that of other women (and many men) to include the addition of other women's rights beyond that of the right to vote.

MAHATMA GANDHI

"Our task is to make the impossible possible." Mahatma Gandhi

The context for the Profile of Mahatma Gandhi is India under the rule of the British Establishment. Indian citizens were treated as inferior to the English, even to the point of denying them their human rights and sacrificing them for their personal desires and needs. A sense of British superiority pervaded all of India, but was especially evident in the cities and in the military organization in which the British served as powerful administrators. The British Establishment could have annihilated groups or individuals who threatened, proposed or attempted an overthrow of the government. However, they underestimated the growing and pervasive power of nonviolence among the eastern Indians. It was in this oppressive setting that Mahatma Gandhi sought truth, love for others (even enemies) and freedom through nonviolent activity.

Gandhi's approach to nonviolent political action has become known throughout the world and has influenced large numbers of people in every social class. Gould (1989) suggests that nonviolence may be the most revolutionary idea of the twentieth century. Gandhi's particular emphasis upon the fundamental right to life, which is both protected and reinforced through non-violence, has been the means used in many subsequent social reform campaigns in the last century.

Some critics have been suspicious of Gandhi's relationship with people in power, especially with certain British administrators. Supporters argue that these relationships were maintained in order to effect a change of heart, so that the people in power would be inspired to act as trustees for the poor and the powerless. When this approach failed, Gandhi turned to nonviolent civil disobedience. However, his proactive nonviolence did not mean that he condemned confrontation in any form. Indeed, for Gandhi, conflict appeared to be an intrinsic characteristic of society, although he clearly specified that the means for civil disobedience must be as moral as its ends or goals. As such, good ends do not justify evil means. His basic position was that the approach to conflict was also a process of discernment of the Truth through nonviolent or passive resistance (*satyagraha*). Gandhi's conflict was against unjust civil laws that degraded the individual or abused human rights. In South Africa, this meant the abusive law of apartheid, which was applied to eastern Indians as well as to native Africans and the "colored." The parallel in India were civil laws that reflected the belief that some citizens were fundamentally superior to others. These laws were both divisive and oppressive. As such, the laws contradicted Gandhi's fundamental belief in the essential unity of God, who created all humans as equal.

Gandhi developed his *modus agendi* throughout different phases in his life. His basic approach was to focus on some specific form of discrimination, integrate internally the effect of the action, revise his means and then proceed to the next decision. In each of these actions he believed he perceived Truth in progressive stages. Gandhi's first encounter with the law and culture occurred in South Africa where Indians were imported to work in difficult and oftentimes dangerous jobs, such as mining. As a young lawyer, he went to South Africa after an unsuccessful career in India. While on a train, he sat in a compartment for "whites only." Responding to a complaint from a white passenger, the conductor stopped the train and literally threw him off. This incident triggered his first campaign for justice, an attack on the racist apartheid government of South Africa.

In 1906, thousands of east Indians in South Africa followed him in his first act of civil disobedience by burning their passes, which the registration law required them to carry. (Carter, 1995) Gandhi's focus in this case and in subsequent challenges to structural injustice was characterized by a nonviolent, but non-cooperative, attack on laws that he believed did not respect human dignity. (Although he condemned violence, he also stated in a famous quote that he preferred violence to cowardice. [Munschenk, 1989, p.30]) He used this same method in South Africa when the white Afrikaners were in power and in India where the British controlled the government, commerce and culture. It cannot be overstated that he insisted that all human beings *are* equal. This sense of equality established for Gandhi a brotherhood of men, women and children. (Amber, 1989) In a very real sense and consistent with his position, Gandhi condemned unjust laws and structures, but he did not despise the people who administered the system. He recognized that, after all, they too were human beings and members of society. His protest was leveled against the structure of the governing bodies. Gandhi felt that neither the apartheid government of South

Africa nor the British rule in India respected the human rights and the dignity of the person.

Because of his opposition to the rule of law that he believed to be unjust, Gandhi was imprisoned numerous times for his civil disobedience. He felt that each imprisonment increased his insight of the Truth. It also added to his growing moral power and credibility. As stated previously, his basic approach was to take a position on a particular practice, review its effects and incorporate it into his next action. In this sense, Gandhi was not a theorist and certainly not an academic conceptualist, but an effective and thoughtful social activist.

Two alternative approaches can bring about effective change. In the first, the conceptual, (or theoretic) approach that is developed can be applied to reality; in effect, this is a top down, or deductive, approach. Secondly, empirical or practical experience can be tested to produce an effective solution, or what would provide a bottom-up, or inductive, approach. Gandhi applied this second approach in his civil disobedience actions and non-cooperative stance with the Establishment. As he proceeded, testing strategies in a trial and error fashion, Gandhi increased his power to challenge and overturn unjust political structures. He became the champion of human rights and ultimately forced the Establishment to acknowledge, if not embrace, his moral power. His uniqueness laid in his ability to combine moral appeal with shrewd political leadership. (Carter, 1995) As such, he possessed moral power, not political power. (To the contrary, Nehru, his student and successor, seized the opportunity to obtain political power.)

It was Gandhi's moral power that transformed India from a British colony to a free democracy. It is another example of Transforming Justice. Indeed, it could be called *contributive* Transforming Justice in the sense that it was Gandhi's moral power that actually brought about the establishment of an Indian democracy.

Among other actions, two practical applications reflected Gandhi's moral power in the field of commerce that also had political overtones. One was the problem that arose when the English no longer imported indigo to dye their textiles. Indigo was the primary crop for Indian farmers. For many, it was their only source of income, the loss of which meant that farmers could not support their families. Gandhi reacted by asking the Indians to make their own cloth with a spinning wheel and loom at home, in effect boycotting English imports. The English textile market, which depended upon exports to India for its success, became a financial disaster. The boycott was effective.

A second similar incident involved retrieving salt from the Indian Ocean. The Establishment controlled the mining of salt. It was illegal for the citizens to mine salt without permission from the government. Gandhi was the first to disobey the law that prevented ordinary citizens from earning a livelihood. He organized the Salt Tax campaign and the march to Dandi Beach. It was probably more effective than any other campaign to illustrate "the power of Truth." (Ambler, 1989, p. 96.)   Citizens from all different classes and economic status joined in this march.   Many were arrested but the spirit of liberation was not undaunted.   Indeed, the march strengthened Gandhi's resolve to create a free India.

Mahatma Gandhi never resisted arrest related to his acts of civil disobedience.   He believed that such arrests could be effectively incorporated in his plans for further action.   Gandhi took what may be called a "spiral" approach to truth seeking in the social and political forums.   His initial insights led to social action (such as marches), which in turn led to greater insights for further social action.   The spiral would start with an aversion to unjust laws.   Employing civil disobedience, he would be arrested without offering any resistance.   Once incarcerated, he would interact with others to refine his position on a particular social action and prepare for the next nonviolent demonstration.   The March to Dandi Beach became a mechanism for bonding all types of people and members of social classes, since the social issues touched everyone whose livelihood depended upon the use of salt.   These nonviolent protesters became a source of power against the government's monopoly on salt.   It is not clear whether subsequent proponents of nonviolence (such as Martin Luther King, Jr. and Cesar Chavez) technically followed Gandhi's spiral approach to effect change.   The spiral approach could, and did, involve confrontation.   But Gandhi also believed that nonviolent confrontation could be an act of virtue.

For Gandhi, the "true" Indian lived in villages where people had few, if any, material goods besides food, shelter and clothing.   He chose a life of voluntary poverty in order to identify more closely with the poor.   He believed that the fewer possessions a person had, the greater she or he would be included into the communion with other humans.   "Gandhi could say without exaggeration that his all-absorbing goal in life was to seek and to serve God as Truth."   (Iyer, 1989, p.124.)   He believed that through poverty, he could gain greater insight to Truth.   In addition, Gandhi believed that the earth contains enough resources for its population.   He abhorred the insatiable acquisitiveness of capitalism as well as the mechanistic materialism of communism.   He "...sought to purify politics by showing that its sovereign principle is neither coercive nor manipulative power, but rather moral and social progress."   (Iyer, 1989, p.127.)

Throughout his life, Gandhi also withdrew from confrontation when he realized that success could only come from some form of violence or forceful physical means.   Furthermore, " [j]ustice was not to be achieved through power over others, but through power over oneself."   (Smith, 1989, p.113.)   In this way, a person would illustrate the power of Truth.   Indeed, Gandhi's "inner voice" was a privileged disclosure of the Truth.   For him, religion is simply the pursuit of Truth under a different name.   Thus, religion is the means to attain Truth.   Indeed, it is not that God is Truth, but that Truth is God.   The brotherhood of humans allowed for contributions of each religious sect.   Gandhi used to say that he was Hindu, Moslem, Jew and Christian.   He quoted from the texts of each religion at appropriate times.   Although he was a deeply religious person, Gandhi believed that no organized religious sect possessed all the Truth.

The saintly qualities attributed to Gandhi—control over one's passion, voluntary poverty, relationships based on equality of all human beings, the power of nonviolence and other convictions—create a sense of his moral power. In the end his image was partially tarnished by his dogmatism and coercive demands for his point of view.   However, these weaknesses did not directly interfere with his commitment to bring about a change in Indian society. Juergensmeyer (1989, p. 48)) claims that it is Gandhi's approach to nonviolent action "...characterized by *satyagraha* introduces a new moral reality, one to which Gandhi's own personal virtues or lack of them are subordinate." It is Gandhi's moral power in *satyagraha* that exemplifies his contribution to Transforming Justice.

JUDGE FRANK M. JOHNSON JR.,
and
Dr. MARTIN LUTHER KING, JR.

"Judge Frank Johnson is a man who gave meaning to the word 'justice'."
Dr. Martin Luther King, Jr.

The context of the Old South was one in which state laws and city ordinances diminished not only the constitutional rights but, in addition, the human rights of African-American citizens. Segregation was practiced in all venues and at every level of social activity, even in the churches. (Segregation was not limited to churches in the South, however. When one of my colleagues visited East St. Louis in 1948, a Catholic priest at Sunday Mass bellowed: "You niggers go to your own churches, not to those for white people.") The institutionalization of segregation had a legal basis in the 1896 U.S. Supreme Court decision that interpreted the Equal Protection Clause of the Fourteenth Amendment as meaning "separate but equal" in the *Plessy v. Ferguson* case. It should be recalled that the Fourteenth Amendment referred to the states rather than to the federal government. It was the *states* that were to provide equal protection under the law for their citizens. With the Supreme Court ruling the states could legally practice segregation by providing separate facilities in public places, such as restrooms in bus terminals. From my personal experience, equality was unfortunately limited or non-existent in the type, quality and care of public facilities. The practice of segregation was almost universal in the South.

Alabama's Governor George Wallace proclaimed in an impassioned speech that segregation did exist yesterday, does exist now and will exist forever.

The setting for the Profiles of Judge Frank Johnson and Dr. Martin Luther King, Jr. involved three important contextual aspects. First of all, at the time state law maintained and protected widespread segregation in the South. Secondly, Judge Frank Johnson accepted the challenge first to examine and subsequently to override state law and city ordinances with decisions based on constitutional law. The third significant aspect involved the elevated hope of racial equality raised by King's petulant "I have dream" speech that reflected past successes, but also opened possibilities for future action. Jack Bass began his biography of Judge Johnson, *Taming the Storm* (1993, p.1) with these words: "They met only once outside a courtroom setting, a brief encounter on an elevator. But the actions of Frank M. Johnson, Jr. *inside* the courtroom and Martin Luther King, Jr. *outside* it unleashed forces that *transformed* Alabama and the American South, expanded the role of law in American society, and shaped the nation's history." (Emphasis added.)

Both of these men brought change in many areas of society. Johnson reformed the segregated Alabama penal system, while King advanced the role of African-Americans in the workplace. Both men focused upon the same problem: equality in the application of civil rights. Both subscribed to nonviolent methods of achieving their goals. Johnson perpetuated effective change through creative interpretation and application of the law, while King brought about change through demonstrations, rather than through terrorist activity. It was Gandhi's nonviolent approach to social issues that had a great impact upon King. Kilgore (1989) wrote that King's concern for social justice and the employment of nonviolent direct action were rooted in his theological ethics. King's movement of nonviolence drew freely from the thought of Gandhi both at the levels of strategy and tactics. Like Gandhi, King stressed that nonviolence must be active, not merely passive, and directed against unjust systems rather than against the people working within these systems. But King, unlike Gandhi, did not openly incorporate asceticism into his movement.

Various contexts arose in which Johnson and King were in the courtroom within the bar but on different sides of the bench. These are detailed in the following paragraphs. In the end, however, both men had far reaching consequences in the process of developing Transforming Justice. Both had power: Johnson had legal power provided by the U.S. Constitution and its amendments, while King garnered social power over time. Both had rights: Johnson employed his interpretation of the Constitution as the source of his rights, while King believed his rights went beyond unjust civil laws. However, there are three specific occasions on which Johnson and King faced each other in the courtroom and the decisions of the court (legal power) provided the means (social power) for Transforming Justice, at first locally, but then nationally.

The three situations involve the decisions related to the Rosa Parks case, the Freedom Riders and the Selma March. In these three cases Johnson interpreted the Constitution's First and Fourteenth Amendments of freedom of speech, due process and equal protection.

Rosa Parks and the Bus Boycott

On December 1, 1955, Mrs. Rosa Parks, a forty-two year old seamstress accompanied by two friends boarded a bus on Cleveland Street in Montgomery, Alabama. They sat down in the first seats reserved for blacks behind the whites-only section. After a few stops the white bus driver, in compliance with state laws decreeing separation of races, told the three black women to stand and give their seats to newly arrived white passengers. Although her two friends complied, Mrs. Parks, tired from her day's work and carrying heavy packages, refused. The driver called a policeman. Mrs. Parks was arrested, jailed and fined $14. (Kennedy, 1978)   She then telephoned a friend and former NAACP president, E.D. Nixon, who in turn consulted with black ministers in Montgomery, including the young Martin Luther King, Jr. These leaders decided to call a boycott of Montgomery buses. About 30,000 blacks participated in the boycott, which lasted 385 days. About 200 black drivers used private cars and vans to transport people. The city used every conceivable ploy to harass and to arrest the owners, drivers and riders, including Dr. King himself. (Kennedy, 1978) It is estimated that the income of the city transit line had dropped over 65% during the period of the boycott.

Mrs. Parks entered a suit in federal court. When this case became bogged down in the state courts, the case was heard by the three-judge District Court, which also heard constitutional challenges to state laws. Judge Frank Johnson was one of these judges. Appeals from this court went directly to the Supreme Court. The case became that of *Browder v. Gayle*. Browder was one of the four black plaintiffs and the white Mayor Gayle was the first of nine defendants.

After the trial and the judges' retirement to chambers, Judge Johnson declared: *"I don't think segregation in any public facilities is constitutional. It violates the equal protection clause of the Fourteenth Amendment...The law will not tolerate discrimination on the basis of race."* (Bass, 1993, p. 110. Italics in original.) Later in an interview with Bill Moyers, Johnson stated: *"There are rarely ever any dramatic moments in a judge's conference room. It's a cold, calculated, legal approach."* (Bass, 1993, p.110. Italics in original.)   Johnson focused on the constitutional issue, which the plaintiffs read with optimism. During the hearing the twenty-seven year-old Dr. King whispered to the Reverend Ralph Abernathy: "It looks as if we might get a favorable verdict." (Bass, 1993, p.110)) This turned out to be true.

In the 1954 *Brown v. Board of Education of Topeka, Kansas*, the U.S. Supreme Court overturned the "separate but equal" doctrine of the 1896 *Plessy v. Ferguson* decision. This verdict applied directly to educational facilities.

Two judges, Johnson and Rivers (creating a majority of two to one) applied the *Brown* decision to the Rosa Parks bus boycott ruling. This result was destined to have far-reaching implications to the entire desegregation movement. (In his writing of the decision in the *Cooper v. Aaron* case, Justice Brennan of the U.S. Supreme Court used the word "desegregation" rather than the word "integration" as it related to schools, since he thought the latter word was too inflammatory for the South.) (Eisler, 1993) The Rivers-Johnson ruling in the Montgomery bus boycott case was the first application of the 1954 school desegregation ruling to a non-school case. It later was applied to the desegregation of all Montgomery parks and public facilities. (Kennedy, 1978) Johnson exercised simplicity and consistency in his thinking: a constitutional right is a constitutional right, no matter in what context it is applied.

Martin Luther King had termed the desegregation of Montgomery buses "...a victory for democracy and the forces of justice." (Yarborough, 1981, p.56) Indeed, the Montgomery bus ruling became the boycott that would become the impetus for the modern revolution in civil rights. (Yarborough, 1981) The Rosa Parks-Montgomery boycott was an application of Transforming Justice in the sense that the legal rights of Parks plus the judicial power of Johnson and the social power of King coalesced into Transforming Justice applied to civil law.

Freedom Riders

In 1961, the Congress of Racial Equality (CORE) and other civil rights groups initiated, under the direction of James Farmer, the Freedom Riders. The goal of this group was to end segregation on interstate buses and to test segregation in bus station waiting rooms, rest rooms and lunch counters. Both the Trailways and Greyhound terminals in Birmingham, Alabama became the locations for white mob violence against black (and some white) passengers. Local police authority took a hands-off approach and stood by without controlling the mob or intervening. The Kennedy administration ordered four hundred federal marshals to Birmingham to regain order. At the request of local civil authorities, Judge Johnson ordered a temporary restraining order against CORE, King and others by banning further organized freedom rides pending a hearing. Judge Johnson stated: "Those who sponsor, finance and encourage [freedom rides] with the knowledge that such publicized trips will foment violence are just as effective in causing obstruction to the movement of *bona fide* interstate bus passengers as are those defendants named in the Government's complaint." (Bass, 1993, p.81) Although Johnson acknowledged the exercise of a legal right, he insisted that the right of the public to be protected was a greater and more important right. Indeed, he warned that he would not hesitate, if required for keeping peace, to put Klansmen, city officials, city policemen and African-American preachers in the Federal penitentiary. King complied, but Farmer did not. The judge was true to his word.

Bass (*Cox News Service*, July 27, 1999) observed: "Although his orders helped transform the social order in the south, Johnson never viewed matters before him as societal issues. To him they were always legal issues." This statement certainly reflects Judge Johnson's position in the Freedom Riders decision. Indeed, he stated in an interview: "My basic philosophy as a trial judge and as an appellate judge is to follow the law and the facts without regard to the consequences." *(NY Times,* July 24, 1999)

Selma

The most recognized and publicized event involving both Judge Johnson and Dr. King was the Selma March. This event also illustrated the deep differences between these two men in terms of the law. They both viewed law as a means to peaceful coexistence. Johnson viewed the law as a means for creating peace among the various constituents. He saw law as serving justice and, therefore, a code that must be obeyed. On the contrary, King saw law as a means to social equality. When state law or city ordinance law actually protected inequality, as in the cases of Rosa Parks and Freedom Riders, King believed that an appropriate goal was to aspire to get the law changed. His means differed from those of Johnson: King believed in non-violent protest, even to the point of civil disobedience to what he perceived to be an ill-conceived or unjust law.

In his decision on segregation, Johnson applied the three constitutional concepts of equal protection (Fourteenth Amendment), due process (First and Fourteenth Amendments) and freedom of speech (First and Fourteenth Amendments). It should be recalled that the First Amendment and the Fifth Amendment applied to the federal government. While the Fourteenth Amendment, as a post-Civil War Amendment, applied to state governments, The Fourteenth Amendment also added the "equal protection under the law" provision that was not directly expressed in the Bill of Rights.

In Selma, county and city officials were confronted daily with marches and demands that discrimination in voter registration be abolished. Selma is located fifty miles west of Montgomery, the Alabama state capitol. King organized a "Freedom March" from Selma to Montgomery to dramatize the demands of blacks to end such voting discrimination. The original march ended in violence. With a temporary injunction against the Alabama government to abandon force against the marches, Johnson held hearings before making a final decision. In a compromise, King and his followers *would* march in defiance of the Johnson's ruling not to march. But they would be turned back peacefully, so violence could be prevented. After the hearing, Johnson's final decision was to permit the march from Selma to Montgomery with certain restrictions. Johnson declared: "The law is clear that the right to petition one's government for the redress of grievances may be exercised in large groups. Indeed, where as here, minorities have been harassed, coerced and intimidated, group association may be the only realistic way of exercising such rights." (Bass, 1993, p.250) But

Johnson emphasized that these rights are not necessarily unrestricted. Furthermore, the court must draw a constitutional boundary line between the competing interests of society. In his ruling, Johnson declared:

> In doing so [determining the constitutional boundary line], it seems basic to our constitutional principles that the extent of the right to assemble, demonstrate and march peacefully along the highways and streets in an orderly manner should be commensurate with the enormity of the wrongs that are being protested and petitioned against. In this case, the wrongs are enormous. The extent of the right to demonstrate against these wrongs should be determined accordingly. (Bass, 1993, p.250)

Judge Johnson also felt that his ruling reached the outer limits of what is constitutionally allowed. Although he believed the Selma march could be a disruptive civil disorder, he decided that the constitutional issue of freedom of speech outweighed local order and peace.

Johnson personally did not look favorably upon civil disobedience. He felt that there were legal means to resolve issues. Consequently, he did not agree with King's civil disobedience even if it were non-violent. When asked what he meant by civil disobedience, King replied:

> One must have the inner determination to resist what conscience tells him is evil with all of the strength and courage and zeal that he can muster; at the same time he must not resort to violence or hatred in the process. It is a way of achieving moral ends through moral means, and I would say that the basis of the philosophy of non-violence is the persistent attempt to pursue just ends by engaging in creative nonviolent approaches and never coming to the point of retaliating with violence or using violence as an aggressive weapon in the process. (Bass, 1993, p.247)

Johnson directly confronted King's thesis that unjust laws should be disobeyed: "The philosophy that a person may—if his cause is labeled 'civil rights' or 'states rights'—determine for himself what laws and court decisions are morally right or wrong and either obey or refuse to obey them according to his own determination, is a philosophy that is foreign to our 'rule-of-law' theory of government." (Yarborough, 1981, p.123) In spite of their different views on civil disobedience, Johnson and King respected each other's sincerity and search for true justice. On at least one occasion, King gave Johnson credit by saying that Johnson gave "true meaning to the word justice." (*Capitol Times*, Madison, WI, July 28, 1999.)

Indeed, Judge Johnson ruled in a manner that was consistent and that may be termed color-blind. Although most of his decisions were made to guarantee black citizens of their civil rights, on occasion he did rule against them. In 1978, he ordered Alabama State University, the state's oldest black college, to stop "its practice of discrimination against whites" in hiring faculty and staff. John Hamner wrote in the *Sarasota Herald Tribune*: (August 4, 1999): "Someone said that Frank Johnson made the south over in his own image. That's wrong. He made it over in the image of the Constitution." In other words, he applied *legal* means to effect Transforming Justice.

In essence, Judge Johnson applied legal justice in his rulings. Legal justice properly belongs to distributive justice insofar as, in this case, Judge Johnson "distributes" justice by using his power to rule in favor of one party. As a judge, especially as a federal judge, he represents the full power of the judicial branch of the government. He is expected to use that power in such a manner that the rights of the government as well as civil rights of its citizens are acknowledged and exercised according to law, and ultimately according to the U.S. Constitution. Assuming that the government is expected to be the ultimate guarantor of justice, through the threat of enforcement, it seems that a judge may use the power of the state to "transform" society. Judge Johnson transformed the interpretation of civil rights, including the right to vote, utilize public schools, and ride public transportation in Alabama. In both situations, coercion was necessary to bring about change.

Coercion or force is another dimension of power. In order to bring about Transforming Justice in these cases, the court not only transformed justice through its interpretation of the Constitution by legally removing restrictions on voting and school attendance. It also transformed the actual application of these rulings through some form of coercion. (As will be discussed in the section on power, coercion is not necessarily unethical or immoral.)

In contrast, Dr. Martin Luther King, Jr. exercised Transforming Justice through the nonviolent means of civil disobedience. It might be argued that he foresaw the possibility, or even the probability, of the use of force. However, foresight does not mean that he actually willed coercion. Ethicists term this kind of situation "double effect." A person foresees that the action may have both a good and an evil effect. The person *wills* the good but *permits* the evil. (Critics have strongly challenged this theory for "splitting hairs.")

In summary, both Johnson and King had rights and power. Johnson had rights as a federal judge. King had rights based on the U.S. Constitution: due process, equal protection and freedom of speech. Johnson had legal power and thus exercised *Legal* Transforming Justice. King had social power and thus exercised *Social* Transforming Justice. Together Johnson and King transformed Alabama and, ultimately, the perspective of the United States on the topic of civil rights and the role of African-Americans. Indeed, Johnson and King both exemplified Transforming Justice!

POPE JOHN XXIII

"The past will never return. New situations require new dispositions."
Pope John XXIII

By the early 1960s the Roman Catholic Church had become isolated from the rest of society. Its legislation and regulations forbade interaction with other religious groups. It still contained the vestiges of an absolute monarchy related to the Middle Ages and eschewed the openness of contemporary Western governments. The 1870 Vatican I decree of papal infallibility in faith and morals distinguished, but separated, the Church from other religions. Furthermore, the Vatican itself was reluctantly granted the recognition of an independent political state by traditional governments. This was a far cry from the days of strong, almost overwhelming, social and political power of the past when the papacy reigned almost supreme over Western countries. Over the years, decades and centuries, the Church, especially the Vatican, became an isolated island in the sea of a changing world. Even the more relatively progressive pope, Pius XII, prohibited interfaith activities. John XXIII changed all that. A favorite image for him characterized the Church as not a museum of antiques, but rather as a garden of life.

Elected as a transitional pope to continue the traditional policies and practices of his predecessor, Pius XII, the seventy-six year old diplomat and Patriarch of Venice, Angelo Roncalli, surprisingly took the name of Pope John XXIII. The previous Pope John XXIII (1410-1415) was an historical disaster, as far as the papacy was concerned; in fact, he was considered one of the anti-popes. The other twenty-two popes named John were legitimate but had short reigns. John was a perfect name for a "transitional" pope. Regardless, when John XXIII convened a council known as Vatican II, he transformed the role of the Roman Catholic Church within itself and in the world. This transformation occurred both within (*ad intra*) and outside (*ad extra*) the Church through the convocation of the Second Vatican Council. (McGrath, 1986; Suenens, 1986.) As pope, he had conferred upon him all the rights and all the power that were granted by Canon Law, that is, church law. This included the infallibility in faith and morals that had been granted to the popes in Vatican I.

The convocation of Vatican II, and its subsequent changes in the Roman Catholic Church, had worldwide impact. General de Gaulle called Vatican II "…the greatest event in the twentieth century." The Secretary-General of the United Nations Organization, Charles Malik, wrote that it might be the greatest event in several centuries. (Congar, 1986, p.339) *Time* magazine (December 31, 1962) named Pope John its "Man of the Year" and proclaimed: "To the entire world Pope John has given what neither diplomacy nor science could give: a sense of unity of the human family." (Hebblethwaite, 1985, p. 468)

These were impressive tributes, but they did not reflect the deep *persona* of the Pope. Born a peasant and later a Vatican diplomat to Greece, Bulgaria, Turkey and France, Angelo Roncalli loved the common people of these nations. He became a loving, non-threatening presence to these people. For Roncalli the diplomat, the powerful were only important to him insofar as they respected the rights of their subjects. However, he was careful not to step on the toes of the powerful, especially government officers who could enhance, reduce, or eliminate the rights of citizens, especially Christians. As representative of the Vatican, he had a simplicity that those in power had to acknowledge but had never experienced before in a diplomat. Cahill (2002, p.151) quotes Cardinal Maurice Feltin, the head of the Catholic peace organization called *Pax Christi* (Peace of Christ) and Archbishop of Paris, as he described Angelo Roncalli:

> He was always friendly, understanding, and sought to smooth out difficult problems; but when action was needed, he did not lack decisiveness and firmness of character. His goodness was strong, not soft.   He could, moreover, be subtle, perspicacious, and farsightedness; and I could give plenty of examples of the way he slipped through the grasp of those who sought to exploit him.

From this description by Feltin, Cahill (2002, p.151) wrote; "Here at last is a portrait of Angelo [Roncalli] not as gregarious simpleton but as a good and subtle priest, employing peasant craftiness and his own hard-won worldliness to achieve humane results—a just judgment."

In his first ninety days, Pope John is said to have "flung open the windows of the Vatican." He convoked the council on January 25, 1959.

Commissions had to be formed, committees established, theologians consulted, and bishops proposed items for the agenda. Furthermore, liberal and conservative contributors quarreled over the content of the documents. Pope John became exasperated with the slow, and narrowly defined documents. He literally measured the results of a document with a ruler and complained: "Seven inches of condemnations and one of praise: is that the way to talk to the modern world?" (Cahill, 2002, p. 185) After much mercurial preparation, Vatican II opened on October 11, 1962.

Apart from convoking the Council, John wrote an encyclical (a papal letter) in 1963 titled *Pacem in terris* (*Peace on Earth*). It was directed to all people on earth. It was not limited to Catholics, as most encyclicals had been written in the past. In this encyclical, he almost single-handedly reversed if not the direction, at least the emphasis, of Catholic doctrine on war and peace. (Zahn, 1971) Pope John insisted that mutual trust was the only basis for world peace. He viewed war as contrary to rational reasoning. *Pacem in terris* is still considered to be one of the great documents of all time. (Heer, 1977) The September 11, 2002, the terrorist destruction in New York and Washington has challenged Pope John's ideal of nonviolence. In spite of his commitment to nonviolence, he did acknowledge the existence of the just war theory. In this conceptualization, war may be used as a defensive measure against those who initiate violence against a country and its populace.

Premier Nikita Khrushchev of the Soviet Union perceived Pope John as a man of peace. During the Cuban Missile Crisis, the Pope pleaded with world leaders to negotiate, on every level, to bring about peace. Cahill (2002, p. 206) wrote: "...no Kremlin general could believe that a Catholic president [John F. Kennedy] was preparing war in the face of such a plea; [Pope] John stood patently on neither side of the argument but in the middle." This was proven to be an effective strategy.

In his direction of the Vatican II Council, Pope John focused on a council that would be inclusive, rather than exclusive. The council should recognize the rights of persons, both in communion with the Roman Catholic Church (Latin and Oriental Rites) and those not in complete union, both Christian (Orthodox and Protestants) and non-Christians (including Muslims and Jews). Charity, not doctrinal argumentation, was to be the primary means for unity. The council was to emphasize "union" with or "communion" with Protestants, Orthodox and others rather than their separation or "return" to the Roman Catholic Church. Karol Wojtyla, as Archbishop of Krakow at the council and later as Pope John Paul II, also insisted on "communion" with members of non-Roman Catholic religions.

The outcomes of Vatican II had three basic components: 1) to maintain a positive and non-condemnatory stance to others who disagree with the doctrine and practices of the Roman Catholic Church; 2) to remain renewing, optimistic and forward-looking; and 3) to act in a way that is pastoral and ecumenical, as opposed to doctrinal as such declared in Vatican I. Pope John wanted the council to provide the rationale — scriptural, theological, philosophical, sociological and psychological — for the role of the Church in contemporary society. According to Christiansen (1984, p 653), he provided "…an egalitarian momentum for modern Catholic social teaching, by redefining the content of the common good in distributional terms." In a word, the Church was to *share* rather than *acquire*. John envisioned the council as an *aggiornamento,* that is, an ongoing updating of the Church to the world. (Capovilla, 1986)

The council was to investigate, recognize and postulate the rights for religious freedom, worship according to one's own religious beliefs, and religious education and corresponding rights needed to operate in contemporary society. (Vatican II, *Pastoral Constitution on the Church in the Modern World*, 1965, #73) John wanted the council to show that the Church is *of* humanity *for* humanity. (Capovilla, 1986) However, rights, including religious rights, are given to persons for exercising their choices. Error, as such, has no rights; people have rights. This concept was, and still is, a controversial issue. Thus, human beings, whether in communion with Rome or not, have a right to worship without coercion by state or society. (Vatican II, *Church in the Modern World*, 1965, #76)

John XXIII used his papal power to establish a council that reflected his beliefs, convictions and desires in accordance with the doctrine of the Roman Catholic Church. To convoke a council that was positive and proactive and not negatively critical, disciplinary or obstructive was within his power as Pope. Papal power is unique. No other sovereign enjoys this kind power. While not absolute, it is limited only by declared doctrine and morals and by Canon Law (that of the Roman Catholic Church). However, the use of papal power is discretionary; it can, and perhaps should, be exercised differently in different situations. Congar (1986, p.137) wrote that in Vatican II: "The vocabulary of 'power' was not employed. The participants spoke rather of mission and service." Perhaps these words imply a power to do good rather than a force to root out evil. The words "mission" and "service" connote a deep commitment to achieve a cause or goal. This in itself is a use of power. Using his papal power to guide the Council in areas of concern for the Church and society, especially the rights and dignity of all people, John XXIII exemplified the epitome of Transforming Justice. He positively transformed the relationship of the Roman Catholic Church with society and with other religious groups. This can be termed *Ecumenical* Transforming Justice.

Was Pope John directly "inspired" by the Holy Spirit, as he claimed? Hebblethwaite (1984) challenges the notion of "direct" inspiration. This issue cannot, and will not, be resolved in this presentation, although it is difficult to argue that this council was not an inspired idea. It was when he was the papal presence in Bulgaria, Greece and Turkey that he experienced first hand the problems of resolving the difficulties among Christians. These included Latin

Roman Catholics, Orthodox Christians, and Eastern Rite Catholics. He was also cognizant of the priorities of non-Christians. He came as a "neighbor" to these groups; he knew how to interact with people at a human level. He approached his ministry with humility, rather than as an official intent on "returning people to the fold." These salient experiences with people's differences in the Mid-east remained in his memory and he felt the need to resolve them. (Hoffmann, 1989) When experiences of this kind are seen within a broader context, they "gel" into a theory or practice. For example, when I give a speech to a professional group, such as the Society for Business Ethics, I have different concepts from research and interaction with colleagues that, as such, are not related to each other. After reviewing them many times, I begin to perceive how they, in fact, do interact and do form one perspective. They seem to "gel" together as a unified presentation.

As papal nuncio to France, Angelo Roncalli was exposed to the "worker priests" movement that seemed to support some underlying tenets of communism. In the case of Roncalli as Pope John XXIII, it seems that these experiences of the Eastern churches and with non-Christians and the "worker priests" of France "gelled" into an inspiration, whether divine or sparked by his human creativity. He called for an ecumenical council that would recognize and deal with these and other problems of contemporary society. Regardless of how the decision to convoke the Council developed, Pope John always saw the "finger of God" in his actions. (Hebblethwaite, 1984.) However, Komonehak (2000) claims that by "inspiration" Pope John did mean that his idea was not entirely his own but that its divine grace was confirmed when he brought the idea to his closest advisors.

Out of this experience, the Pope charged the Council to investigate ecumenism. The World Council of Churches had initiated the ecumenical movement in 1948. It was composed of Protestant and Orthodox churches. The Vatican, under Pius XII, prohibited active participation in both the 1948 and the 1954 meetings. But the Roman Catholic Church changed its approach to those other groups in Vatican II. Hans Küng (1986, p.31) expressed the change: "Being truly Christian today means being an *ecumenical Christian*." (Italics in original.) On May 30, 1960 Pope John XXIII established the Secretariat for the Union of Christians (SPCU). Stransky (1986, p.64) wrote that the SPCU "...ushered in the official entrance of the Roman Catholic church into the one ecumenical movement." Indeed, the SPCU became the eventual sole author of the *Decree on Ecumenism.* (Stransky, 1986, p.71.) The Decree, however, was also to include all people, whether Christian or not. According to Congar (1986, p.137), "'Communion' is a key concept in the ecumenism to Vatican II...." However, the Church is a pilgrim society as well as the new people of God. Protestant observer Bishop John R. H. Moorman (1986) stated that the Decree on Ecumenism marked the entry of Rome into the ecumenical movement. The Roman Church started to emerge from its "closed citadel." Cahill (2002, p.184) perceived the Council in these terms: "The council should meditate upon the

Church not as a juridical institution but as a mystery unfolding in time, a mystery central to the healing of the world."

Twenty years after the closing of Vatican II, Cardinal Joseph Bernadin of Chicago (1986) saw the renewal of the Roman Catholic Church manifested in three areas. These were specifically: 1) collegiality of the bishops, such as shared decision-making; 2) notable impetus towards ecumenical interaction; and 3) spiritual renewal through emphasis on the liturgy, the scriptures and the nature of the Church.

Indeed, in convoking Vatican II, Pope John XXIII moved the Church and contemporary society towards Transforming Justice. Joseph Komonehak (2000) wrote that Pope John had by force of his personality and by charm of his manner demystified the papacy. By unleashing the pent-up movements of renewal and reform, he had begun a *transformation* of the Church. Although Vatican II might be his greatest contribution to the Church and to society, there are several other situations that illustrate Pope John's down-to-earth human qualities that are a legacy to the whole world.

First, Pope John, like many of the Profiled Leaders, acted in a manner that might be considered a breach of civil law. As the Vatican representative to the countries of Greece, Turkey and Bulgaria, he had diplomatic immunity. He used diplomat pouches to provided stacks of "Immigration Certificates" issued by the Palestinian Jewish Agency for distribution to Jews, who were at that time fleeing from Eastern Europe. Cahill (2002, p. 137) wrote: "Out of interventions like these the legend may have arisen that Angelo [Roncalli] actually issued baptismal certificates to save Jews; and though he may have done so, it is far more likely that these were Vatican visas...." Although there are no accurate records of the number of Jews Roncalli assisted, it is estimated that he helped from between 24,000 to 55,000 people to flee from persecution. This is an application of Transforming Justice.

Secondly, after talking with a Vatican City maintenance man, Pope John was appalled at the low salaries of these and other Vatican employees. He immediately doubled their salaries. When some of his staff remarked that this increase in salaries would limit the Vatican's contributions to charity, Pope John responded, without hesitation, that justice comes before charity. This is another example of Transforming Justice. His decision affected the entire Vatican staff.

Amid all turmoil and change, Pope John maintained his humanity. John found the delaying tactics of the governing body of the Church and others in preparation for the Council exasperating. When a visitor asked him how many people work at the Vatican, he replied: "About half." (Cahill, 2002, p. 198.) He had a sense of humor that is not easily observed in other Profiled Leaders. Another example of Pope John XXIII *the person* came when he received Jacqueline Bouvier Kennedy, the wife of President Kennedy, in a private audience. Protocol required that he call her "Mrs. Kennedy" or "Madame," since their conversation was to be in French. But when he saw this exquisite woman coming toward him, he opened his arms and exclaimed, "Jackie!". (Cahill, 2002, p. 187-188.)

Not only did John XXIII transform the Catholic Church, he also transformed the attitude of Christians and non-Christians towards the papacy. Here was a pope of the people, not of the establishment. For Cahill (2002, p.175) "Here at last was a pope as a pope ought to be." Everyone except the ruling body of the Roman Church, the Rota, loved John XXIII. Perhaps, just perhaps, it was the *persona* of Pope John, rather than Vatican Council II and the encyclical *Pacem in terris*, that transformed the Roman Catholic Church. His popularity in Rome as a holy man is unquestionable. *Vox populi*, or the voice of the people, was clearly heard when Pope John Paul II beatified him. This is just one step away from declaring him a saint! The common people, whom he loved dearly, reciprocate that love when they refer to him as *Good Pope John*.

CESAR CHAVEZ

"Nothing changes until the individual changes." Cesar Chavez

In the early 1900s, the legal status of the migrant worker was extremely limited. California state law prohibited men, women and children to unionize. It was almost impossible to challenge the farmers (and owners) who had enough political, economic and social power to control the living conditions, education and working environment of the migrant workers. Additionally, the heavy use of pesticides made the working conditions in the fields hazardous. The establishment, including some of the churches, was suspicious of these uneducated, non-English speaking, poor and needy migrants. Racial profiling was common. This was the setting in which Cesar Chavez began what became akin to his ministry, eclipsing his simple role as a social activist.

Chavez had little formal education because of the constant movement of his own migrant parents from farm to farm. His natural intelligence led to a program of self-education. He was especially interested to read the writings on the nonviolent protests and the fasting of Gandhi. The influence of Gandhi on Martin Luther King, Jr. also impressed Chavez. This intellectual discovery led Cesar Chavez to dedicate his life to a fight against social injustice modeled upon then nonviolent methods of Gandhi and Martin Luther King, Jr. Specifically, he emulated Gandhi's example by fasting. (Hammerback, 1998) He focused his mission on the plight of the migrant worker and made this his highest priority. Chavez became a national figure, as founder and president of the United Farm Workers Union in the 1960s. The union was at its strongest in the 1970s with a membership of 50,000. His crusade began with unionization of poorly paid migrant workers with the goal of liberating them from squalid working and living conditions. He fought for a minimum wage law. In the 1970s, he initiated successful consumer boycotts of grapes and iceberg lettuce. These boycotts occasioned a nationwide impetus for social change. His nonviolent approach directed toward the formation of a union differed appreciably from the violent tactics of some other unions.

Chavez was a firm believer in the irreversibility of social change: once it is started, it leads to further change. He patterned his approach after the civil rights movement in the United States. Through the unionization of workers in the agriculture industry, notably the migrant workers, he fought for a change in the contract between the farmer employer and the low-paid employee. The traditional inequality of power between employer and employee, while not eliminated, became more balanced. He was successful in making over 100 contracts with various California growers. His opponents were the California Farm Bureau, the California Grape and Fruit Tree Fruit League, the South Central Farmers Committee, and Whitaker and Baxter, a San Francisco public relations firm hired by the growers. (Hammerback, 1998) He showed his opposition to these powerful forces through a hunger strike that produced a successful nation-wide grape boycott. His power to bring about change increased and developed over many years of periodic fasting, boycotts and marches. Chavez stated that power is what is important; all depends on how the power is used. Hammerback (1998, p.19) quoted Chavez: "I soon realized that you can't do anything by talking, that you can't do anything if you haven't got the power...Now I seldom like to go see my opponent unless I have some power over him." This use of power became a type of Transforming Justice.

Chavez fought for civil rights. California's Agricultural Labor Relations Act of 1975 gave farm workers the right to collective bargaining, which they previously did not experience. This landmark legislation serves as a memorial to the efforts of Cesar Chavez. However, his fundamental position and philosophy was that the weak have no rights except the right to sacrifice until they are strong (*i.e.*, powerful). He realized that the weak, as disenfranchised, had to attain power to bring about change. Chavez introduced the concept of the "Synanon Game" which encouraged self-criticism and enabled the laborers to identify their loyalties. (Mills, 1993) Furthermore, he believed that personal contact with its members was essential to form a successful organization. All of these means were a reflection of Gandhi's approach to social change. Although some authors attribute Chavez's success to his charismatic personality (Nelson, 1966; Dunne 1967; Mathiessen, 1969) or his rhetorical qualities (Hammerback, 1998), others claim that his strategy and tactics were more effective than those of his opponents, which included both the growers and the competing AFL-CIO union (Ganz, 2000). According to Ganz, (2000, p. 1005) "[d]ifferences in strategic capacity can explain how resourcefulness compensates for each of resources when insurgent social movements overcome more powerful opponents." Strategy is the means one has to attain the focal goal. It is probable that leaders of new organizations, such as the United Farm Workers Union, have more strategic capacity and flexibility than leaders of more established organizations, which are bound by institutionalized routines, practices and unwritten rules. Chavez believed that the AFL-CIO fell into this category.

Once workers had the right to collective bargaining, Chavez turned his attention to environmental considerations in the workplace. (Gordon, 1999) He used nonviolent means to make people aware of hazardous working conditions confronting the migrants. He wanted employees protected from the cancer-causing risks of unregulated pesticides, such as captan, parathion and methyl bromide. Regulations passed in 1992 (just prior to Chavez's death in 1993) mandate pesticide manufacturers to label all products in accordance with the law. Furthermore, growers are now required by law to supply workers with protective clothing and adequate bathing and emergency safety facilities. This policy attempts to balance the interests and power between growers and laborers. Indeed, these decisive actions of Chavez demonstrate applications of Transforming Justice.

Like some of the other Profiled Leaders who illustrated Transforming Justice, Chavez had his personal weaknesses. His insistence on absolute and total control over the organization and his overemphasis on boycotts eventually weakened the strong power of the United Farm Workers. He gradually became isolated from the union members, exercising nepotism in the hiring of incompetent family members to manage aspects of the union, and ceased to engage in face-to-face personal contact to obtain commitment and retain loyalty from the workers. (Bardache, 1993; Hammerback, 1998) The positive promotion of other labor unions (like the Teamsters) directly reduced the power of the United Farm Workers as organizers and indirectly affected the control that Chavez had over them.

On a personal level, Chavez lived a simple and profoundly spiritual life. Through his example of service, nonviolence, leadership and humility, he has been dubbed a modern-day saint, akin to Mother Theresa of Calcutta. Through his spirituality and nonviolence, he became a "transformer" by empowering the migrant workers.

In many respects, Chavez's spirituality reflected more the Christian orientation of Martin Luther King, Jr. rather than the Hindu underpinnings of Gandhi. Both King and Chavez had strong ties to organized religion. On the contrary, Gandhi had no commitment to any particular theological or philosophical ideology. Gandhi believed that nonviolence and renunciation in and of themselves comprised the highest form of religion. Gandhi relied on self-purification through prayer and fasting to bring about social change. Martin Luther King, Jr., on the other hand, found government programs to be a vehicle for social change. Gandhi pursued the notion that God is Truth. He was a deeply spiritual person. Like Gandhi, Chavez was also a deeply religious man. His many fasts and love of voluntary poverty were manifestations of his personal piety. He also used the Roman Catholic Mass to initiate his major initiatives. Indeed, his humble manner and efforts combined the idealism of Roman Catholic social teaching with the nonviolent movements of Gandhi and King.

Chavez, it seems, combined the two approaches of Gandhi and King to develop a social justice based on the principles and practices of organized religion. It might be said that Chavez translated his religious convictions into secular actions. If this is true, as I believe it is, then he opened the door to a religious, as well as a spiritual, dimension to Transforming Justice. The "justice" here is a type of social justice. The means and the power came from the application of the Catholic social teaching, specifically on social issues such as the right to form unions, as illustrated by the United Farm Workers.

The most publicized and dramatic example of the advancing of the farm workers' cause occurred in their twenty-one day, 250-mile march from Delano (the headquarters of the United Farm Workers) to Sacramento (California state capitol) in 1966. Similar to Gandhi's Salt March and King's Selma March, this action brought together and unified people, both groups and individuals, who would not ordinarily interact. Marchers included farm workers, religious leaders, educators, social workers and other activists, thus creating a solidarity among the participants. Interestingly, as the original group proceeded to Sacramento, additional small groups of farm workers would join in the march. By the time the marchers reached Sacramento, the number had swelled to approximately 10,000 participants. Unlike Gandhi's Salt March and Martin Luther King, Jr.'s Selma March, Chavez's Delano-Sacramento March incorporated a religious dimension. Mexican Catholic culture, in which bare-foot walking and penance is not uncommon, made the march assume the character of a religious procession. (In a similar manner, Hispanic Chicagoans in the Pilsen neighborhood fasted and marched in 2001 to protest the postponed decision of the school board to build a new high school nearby. Chavez lives on!)

Power in this kind of Transforming Justice comes from the union of like-minded persons, in this case the migrant workers. This power is directly dependent upon the group dynamic of the membership. The more united the individuals, the greater is their power to bring about change. Unlike the power of Gandhi and King, which became internationally recognized and applied, the power of Chavez was almost exclusively directed to bring justice to local migrant workers. Nonetheless, the boycotts of grapes and iceberg lettuce did have national recognition, as stated above. Chavez almost instinctively knew that power lay in changing people. He believed that people were changed by doing rather than by theorizing. In essence, he applied and succeeded by adhering the adage that "actions speak louder than words".

Chavez, like other transforming leaders such as Gandhi and King, insisted that human rights were the first priority. Once human rights were acknowledged by society, civil (legal) rights followed. Chavez's actions exemplify a clear process. The first step is to establish human rights. Next, power is developed through the union of like-minded persons. Finally, this power is applied to situations that can initiate change. The change can occur as an individual action (such as negotiating a contract with a single grower) or through a legal ordinance (such as the Labor Relations Act of 1975). Chavez created a coalition that led to the signing of 150 contracts with table grape growers in 1970. However, by 1973 working conditions for migrants had not improved significantly. Chavez then chose to publicize the dangerous environmental situation that existed in the fields. This strategy ultimately attracted additional mainstream support.

Arizona (where Chavez was born) and California (where he formed the United Farm Workers), as well as other localities, have established a Cezar Chavez Memorial Day on his birthday, March 31. In 1996 on the third anniversary of his death, 50 separate events spanning six states memorialized his passing and reflected his influence on many facets of society. (Rodebaugh, 1996) His actions are acknowledged as a model for the process of obtaining social justice. He also exemplified Transforming Justice in the use of rights and power to bring about change in the lot of migrant farm workers. He implemented in a very concrete situation the concept of Transforming Justice.

NELSON MANDELA

"Instead of growing old and irrelevant, Mandela grew into a myth." Freemantle

In some respects, Nelson Mandela faced a challenge that was similar to, but not identical with, that faced by Gandhi. Both men challenged the political and legal power of the State. Gandhi faced the multi-faceted power of the British Establishment, while Mandela contested the basic premise of Afrikaner apartheid. Both men encountered situations that precipitated the use of civil disobedience. Both used nonviolence to attain power. Both had to confront and placate their followers who proposed more violent courses of action. Mandela faced opposition from some South African blacks and colored who favored terrorism and other kinds of violence. Gandhi had to resolve the Muslim-Hindu conflict, as well as Nehru's advocacy of violence.

Mandela had to face an additional problem. The South African administrators believed that by separating Mandela from the public as a prisoner on Robbin Island, they could apply the "out-of-sight, out-of-mind" approach to his growing popularity among non-Afrikaners. This strategy proved to be incorrect. Their psychological warfare failed. While his internment in prison was physically demanding, but not physically damaging, it was philosophically liberating. The same cannot be said of the lot of many of Mandela's followers. Many of his followers were uneducated laborers. They worked in labor-intensive jobs, such as mining. Foreign companies started to move out of South Africa as the apartheid issue increasingly affected their businesses, their employment practices and their investments in a negative way. The United Nations also pressured the government to eliminate apartheid. South Africa gradually fell into social disarray. Blacks took a position against whites, whites against blacks, blacks against blacks, whites against whites. This was the setting for Mandela's rise to power.

Two autobiographies (1994, 1996) and a recent biography by the English author Anthony Sampson (1999) provide detail of the historical development of Mandela's goal to replace Afrikaner apartheid. These authors describe Mandela's goal of attaining a multi-social, multi-cultural, multi-lingual, multi-religious and multi-political South African democracy. More recently, S. Prakash Sethi and Oliver Williams (2001) have given thorough treatment to the change in South Africa in terms of a political, social and religious experience.

Apartheid, as perceived by Prime Minister Hendrick Verword, was based on ethnicity.

> Ethnicity, he explained...was the way of human nature, and any attempt to create a multi-racial nation was not only fallacious but deadly dangerous. Apartheid, by contrast, was the way of liberation: each ethnic 'nation' had a God-given right to its own identity and its own country, and so the white South Africans were prepared to give each black nation its own homeland even as they claimed their own for themselves. (Sparks, 1999, p.74)

As expected, Mandela (1996, p.48) perceived apartheid differently: "Apartheid was designed to divide racial groups...."

The purpose of this presentation is to select and highlight certain aspects of Mandela's philosophy and political thought as they contribute to Transforming Justice. As he matured, especially during his 27 years in prison — most of them on Robbin Island — his approach became less confrontational and more conciliatory. He focused on his goal of equality for all — blacks, colored, whites and even communists. In other words, while his goal remained basically unchanged, his means to that goal shifted dramatically. Sparks (1999) concluded that Mandela achieved his goal to a degree — but not completely.

As a follower of Gandhi, Mandela originally subscribed to nonviolent means, as did Martin Luther King, Jr. However, Mandela viewed nonviolence differently from Gandhi. He wrote (1994, p.174): "I saw nonviolence on the Gandhi model not as an inviolable principle...but as a tactic to be used as the situation demanded." Like Gandhi, Martin Luther King, Jr. and Susan B. Anthony, his first tactics were to employ nonviolent civil disobedience. Strikes, boycotts, non-cooperation with civil authorities and other nonviolent activities were the original means he used to overturn apartheid. These actions became the source of the power that he needed to effect Transforming Justice.

Mandela acknowledged that these nonviolent actions did not always contribute to his goal. He then reluctantly capitulated to the demands of his political party, the African National Congress (ANC), to incorporate limited violence. Sethi-Williams (2001, p.43) wrote: "For most Blacks, the ANC had come to symbolize the struggle for freedom against oppression." As their leader, he permitted guerilla warfare, but he denounced terrorism. The ANC violence, according to some of its leaders, began in the 1960s only in response to the government's own violence (Sethi-Williams, 2001). Mandela believed that terrorism would create a bloody civil war between the extremists on both sides. He utilized resources from many political venues. He incorporated the guerilla warfare of Fidel Castro with his nonviolent actions. Sampson (1999, p.152) wrote: "He would never lose his admiration for Castro." He received money and war material from African countries that denounced apartheid. He even accepted help from governments that violated human rights.

Mandela followed a middle-of-the-road approach to democracy. By doing this, he thus alienated both ultraconservatives and extreme liberals in South Africa. Mandela sought to develop a decentralized political system that was based on the Swiss confederation rather than on American democracy. (Kendall, 1987) In spite of Mandela's efforts, the South African apartheid government almost succeeded in dividing Mandela's goal of an interracial democracy by pitting groups of political activists against each other. (Sampson, 1999)

Critics challenged the means Mandela used for obtaining a democratic society that endorsed racial and economic equality. First, they accused him of violating his commitment to nonviolence when he permitted guerilla warfare. Then critics chastised him, a lawyer, for assisting his white jailors. The jailors came for legal advice and Mandela willingly gave it to them. His critics did not realize that these actions became one of Mandela's means for communicating with his followers on the outside. After the installation of democracy, others claimed that Mandela sold out to the former South African government. He eliminated the death penalty and capital punishment for those administrators who had committed heinous crimes that the apartheid government permitted and even encouraged. (Sampson, 1999) In spite of these and other shortcomings, all, both friends and foe, agree that he was, and still is, a charismatic political figure. (Mitchell, 1997)

Mandela's early experience with capitalism was negative. He was an indentured servant, a modern-day "slave," before seeking and obtaining a formal education. Although he did not reject capitalism outright, he believed that property belonged "to the people." He insisted that equality meant that there should not be institutionalized legal, social and economic differences between those who had economic power, and those who had little— "the haves" and " the have-nots."

Although Mandela personally rejected communism, he did favor, but did not endorse, the socialism of the Scandinavian countries. One of the reasons for the Afrikaner government's denunciation of Mandela was that his social movement (ANC) included blacks, the colored, communists, Indians and some whites. In addition, the pro-African group (PAC) challenged his open policy as a capitulation to world domination by whites. They wanted an exclusively black South African government, as it had been before the English and the Dutch took possession of the country. It should be recalled that rival black tribes originally occupied South Africa. The whites recognized opportunities for economic development. At first, they established corporations that excavated diamonds and coal. Then they diversified. They hired blacks at below a minimum living wage. The Dutch converted the fertile land into productive farms. Foreign companies established profitable subsidiaries in South Africa, using labor with extremely low wages and few benefits. Health insurance, education and other social services were limited to counter these problems. Mandela first proposed working conditions that respected the human rights of the employees. Civil rights came later. (Weld, 1998) He passionately pursued these human rights. They were the underpinnings for his personal application of Transforming Justice.

Foreign investors gradually acknowledged the injustice of South African policies and practices. The Reverend Leon Sullivan, an African-American member of the General Motors Corporation board of directors, developed principles that provided gradual steps to reduce and then, ultimately, to eliminate the racial discrimination that existed in the treatment of black and white employees. They were called the Sullivan Principles. The application of these principles was voluntary. The Sullivan principles were directed primarily toward American companies that had manufacturing operations in South Africa. However, they did not change the Afrikaner policy toward blacks and colored in the workplace. After years of promoting these principles, Sullivan realized that accommodation would not work. He then strongly advocated the withdrawal of American businesses from South Africa. Most American firms through pressure from their own stockholders, gradually complied with his plea. As a result, South Africa's primarily white-based economy suffered. The South African establishment had to adapt to this change of attitude by foreign governments (e.g., no loans), companies (e.g., withdrawal) and society in general (e.g., United Nations censorship of apartheid). Change in the political sphere also seemed inevitable.

Although Mandela did not favor liberal, free market capitalism as such, he realized that some of its policies and practices ultimately could, and most probably would, lead to political, economic and social change in South Africa. He saw the advantages of capitalism, but he was also aware of its defects. He did not approve of what might be termed "American imperialism." Sampson (1999, p. 126) wrote: "Mandela... stated that the future of South Africa was in the hands of the common people functioning in their mass movements."

The South African banks were being seriously affected by the West, which required more equality than the limited rights granted by the Afrikaner government. As stated previously, the Western investors withdrew funds or decided to leave South Africa when they realized that apartheid was no longer financially stable. Some even considered apartheid to be immoral. In order to survive, the Afrikaner government had to submit to a change that acknowledged and protected the civil rights of the minorities. It did so only slowly and grudgingly. Finally, the government realized that without shared power with the blacks, South Africa would be divided by a vicious civil war, or might even cease to exist as an independent nation. In 1986, the strong condemnation of apartheid by the United Nations Organization (UNO) helped to bring about change. This UNO position influenced the actions of member countries. For example, the United States Congress overrode President Reagan's veto of the Comprehensive Anti-Apartheid Act (H.R. 4868). Even conservative leaders like Margaret Thatcher in England and Ronald Reagan in the United States gradually — very gradually — acknowledged the need to accept a shared-power government in South Africa. Thatcher had previously stated that Mandela was a communist. She held this conviction until the end of the Cold War, the fall of the Berlin Wall and its subsequent impact on Soviet-controlled countries. After these events, the threat of a communist takeover in South Africa was no longer a concern. (Sampson, 1999)

President George Bush issued Executive Order 2769 (July 10, 1991) that repealed U.S. sanctions against South Africa. The ANC was concerned because for them sanctions were viewed "...as a crucial indication of political support while the organization pushed the South African government toward the adoption of a democratic constitution." (Sethi-Williams, 2001, p. 346) Mandela argued that it was too early to lift the sanctions.

The South African government finally capitulated to a "shared power" structure comprised of white Afrikaners and the black challengers. Each side had demands, but was also willing to compromise. While the goal of a unified South African was clear, the means were not. There were, and still are, many issues that have to be resolved before Mandela's dream of a multi-racial, multi-cultural, multi-lingual, multi-religious, multi-social and multi-political democratic nation becomes a reality. (Sparks, 1999)

Freemantle (1999, p.17) in his review of Sampson's (1999) *Mandela: The Authorized Biography* wrote:

> As British Anthony Sampson so compellingly demonstrates in the authorized biography Mandela, instead of growing old and irrelevant, Mandela grew into a myth. Instead of fading into leaderless obscurity, the ANC grew into a sophisticated political force, with highly intelligent and educated leaders at the helm. Instead of tearing itself apart, it emerged 27 years later as the only organization with the power to stop the bloodletting and start building a nation.

Mandela exercised political power to bring about change. This could be called *Political* Transforming Justice. He institutionalized human rights in government so that they became civil rights. He fulfilled the conditions for Transforming Justice. Human rights were clearly his goal. Power was gradually developed. Ultimately, this moved a divided country towards justice.

AARON FEUERSTEIN

"Not a fool, not a saint." Thomas Teal

The Northeastern portion of the United States has historically been considered an appropriate location for the textile industry. Initially, labor was cheap and plentiful, while production costs were relatively low. The distribution network was efficient, especially along the Atlantic coast with its large cities like Boston, New York, Philadelphia and Baltimore. However, this environment changed dramatically after World War II. The labor unions made great progress in enlisting the textile workers for better wages and benefits. Machinery that was once "state-of-the-art" became obsolete and had to be replaced with more modern, labor-saving, expensive equipment. Jobs became limited. A fifth of the local population was on welfare. (McCurry, 1997) Workers moved to locations where jobs were more plentiful. Many textile companies moved their plants to the Southeast, where states had "right to work" laws. Unions found it difficult, if not almost impossible, to attract members in the Southeast, partially because they were thought to be "carpetbaggers" who came from the North to invade the South. The 1964 U.S. Supreme Court *Textile Workers of America v. Darlington Manufacturing Company* (380 U.S. 263, 85S.Ct. 994, 136. Ed. 2d 827 [1965]) decision exemplifies confrontation. This decision made it clear that an owner may shut down his or her entire business, but could not close one plant to prevent the unionization of other plants in a holding company. In spite of their differences on the rights of labor, Roger Milliken, the owner of the Darlington Manufacturing Company and twenty-seven other textile plants, had become a friend of Feuerstein. This was the setting for textile owner Aaron Feuerstein as he watched his "labor of love" burn to the ground.

The story began on December 11, 1995, when a fire destroyed the four buildings of the largest textile manufacturing company in the Northeast, the Malden Mills. Thirty-three employees were injured. The structural loss was a complex that measured 750,000 square feet. As the owner, CEO and president of the company, Aaron Feuerstein, as he watched the buildings go up in flames, conceived a plan to mitigate the harmful effects of this fire on his employees. First, he sought the personnel files of the injured employees, so that he personally could inform the families of their injured relative. Next he had to decide whether the company still had a future in the city of Lawrence, Massachusetts. Lawrence was formerly the center of the Northeast textile industry. Malden Mills had become the largest employer in the city. The mills provided jobs for over 2,800 employees in a job-depressed area. Feuerstein's concern for his employees is on the other end of the spectrum from the decision-makers of Enron, Arthur Anderson and other companies that the Security and Exchange Commission (SEC) alleges made illegal transfers of stock, among other felonies.

Malden Mills had developed weight insulating materials (Polartec and Polarfleece) that were used in clothing made by such successful sport and recreational retailers as L.L. Bean, Lands' End, Eddie Bauer and other respected outfitters. The military used these fabrics in some of their gear. Even European textile manufacturers used these products in their sportswear. These two textile products counted for $300 million or 25% of Malden Mills sales in 1995. Malden Mills needed to get the production of these products back to a competitive level for its own survival. (Teal, 1996) Time was of the essence. The problem was that Feuerstein did not have a patent on these products. Competing firms could legally produce them during the rebuilding of Malden Mills.

Aaron Feuerstein faced a number of alternative choices. First, he could collect the $300 million dollars in insurance compensation and walk away from the business, leaving his unionized employees without jobs. The closing of the mills would have a devastating effect on the city for two basic reasons: jobs and taxes. For its own survival, the city of Lawrence needed the Malden Mills to remain open. Furthermore, the mills paid some of the highest wages and benefits ($15/hour) in the region. It was tempting for Feuerstein, who was approaching seventy years of age, to close shop, collect the insurance and take retirement. He rejected this option.

Feuerstein had a second choice. He could reestablish the company in the Southeast, where many of the textile mills relocated because competition for jobs and lower salaries made the area attractive. Unions were an anathema in the South especially in the textile industry; as they were primarily a northern phenomenon. One of the problems with this choice would be the fact that the employees in the South were not skilled in the production of Malden Mills' products. Its state-of-the-art products required proficient workers. To build a new plant and to train employees would allow more time for competitors to capture this attractive market. Training new employees might prove even more difficult because these Southern workers tended not to have a high school diploma. Malden Mills would probably lose its competitive edge in a move to the South. Some business executives, managers and business school professors thought that this choice would be most in accord with contemporary business practices.

Feuerstein had a third alternative choice. He could sell the company to another corporation. But who would want a burned-out plant, in spite of its high-demand products? The popular product lines could not be immediately manufactured and marketed.

A fourth possible option was to sell the company to the employees, as was done in the case of United Airlines, Avis and Weirton Steel. An important criterion for this option is that the employees have sufficient financial stability to purchase the company and the management skills to keep the firm operating. This was doubtful in the case of Malden Mills.

As he watched his family business incinerate in flames, Aaron Feuerstein rejected all the above options. He decided to rebuild Malden Mills, which may be considered either saintly or foolish. It was neither. At the time it seemed to be an astute business decision. It was an unprecedented application of business ethics and social responsibility. Some might term it philanthropy. It was not. It was an intelligent business decision that manifested moral imagination. (Moral imagination will be discussed in Observations in Chapter 4.) Business leaders and ethicists praised Feuerstein for his stand. Colleges and universities bestowed honorary doctorates on him in recognition of his strong moral stance.

Feuerstein decided to rebuild the buildings with his insurance money. If he chose to move to the Southeast, he probably would not have received complete coverage, according to one source. (Teal, 1996) More importantly, he promised to pay his employees their full wages, health insurance, and bonuses until the plant was again operable. This decision cost Malden Mills, a privately held company, $25 million. As owner of the company, Feuerstein could make this decision without consultation with or opposition from shareholders. This decision stunned the business world. But it also created an unprecedented loyalty from his employees. Sunoo (1999, p. 59) wrote: "For 93 years, change (at Malden Mills) has been ever constant. Simultaneously, Malden's employer-employee loyalty has driven the company's life span...(these relationships are) as solid as a brick." This was a positive use of *economic* power. Furthermore, it was the use of economic power that exemplifies Transforming Justice.

One photograph in the media showed the employees carrying Feuerstein on their shoulders. The new plant was constructed with state-of-the-art equipment — and it maintained the same skilled employees. They are more loyal now than before the fire. Employee retention has run above 95%. There has never been a strike in this unionized plant. Production after the fire at first was not able to keep up with demand. Profits were higher than ever. The loyalty of the employees was unprecedented, as was the loyalty of the employer. This committed mutual loyalty is a rarity in the contemporary business environment.

This is a case that exemplifies Transforming Justice. As stated above, Transforming Justice can be accomplished through rights plus power. The power was economic and obviously in the hands of Feuerstein. One might question what rights the employees and the city of Lawrence had in this case.

Aristotle tells us that the goal of humans is goodness. But to achieve goodness, justice is one of the components. Justice deals with rights, and a person has a right to achieve goodness. If work is required to achieve the good life, an individual has a right to a job or work. The problem is easy to state but difficult to resolve: If a person has a right to work in order to obtain a decent life or standard of living, who has the obligation to respect that right? Or, in more practical terms, does a specific company have an ethical, legal or social obligation to hire this particular person? It is not unusual to state that government has the ultimate obligation to provide work for an individual. This is what is generally referred to as distributive justice. Distributive justice will be discussed thoroughly in the section on the components of Transforming Justice in Chapter 3.

But what if a private person chooses to respect this right, as Feuerstein did? Is it justice? This situation seems to be an appropriate example of Transforming Justice. Feuerstein recognized the rights of his employees to the goodness available in life proposed by Aristotle. He fortified their rights with his economic power. He used this power to assure that the plant would be rebuilt. Feuerstein exercised his economic power to guarantee the employees two things. First, he guaranteed their salaries, health benefits and bonuses until the plant was operative. Secondly, he assured the employees that they would still have their jobs when the buildings were rebuilt. In these actions he literally "transformed society," precisely in Lawrence, Massachusetts. His unprecedented decision to provide support beyond the union contract he made with the factory's union became the topic of worldwide discussion, both pro and con. The context was indeed an application of Transforming Justice.

It cannot be proven ethically, legally or business-wise that Feuerstein had an obligation to the employees beyond the usual employer-employee contract. McCurrey (1997, p.34) provides an interesting insight into the Feuerstein legacy: "The third-generation owner of Malden draws much from his grandfathers. His paternal grandfather, the company's founder, instilled in young Aaron a sense of responsibility to his workers. His maternal grandfather, a rabbi, was Feuerstein's guide to Jewish religious learning." In the same article, Feuerstein is quoted: " There's no question that the religious ethical teachings that were inculcated into me in my youth must have played some role in the decision-making to rebuild here."

Not all justice is transforming. Feuerstein used his power to transform the status of the employees, the city of Lawrence and challenged the traditional practices of the textile industry and business in general. His decision also fulfilled Keith Davis and Robert Blomstrom's Social Power Equation: The greater the social power, the greater the social responsibility. (Davis, 1971)

Good ethical decisions in the long run are frequently good business decisions. They produce fewer reasons for cutting corners, producing substandard products and engaging in questionable or even illegal practices that affect competition. However, a businessperson is less likely to be unethical when the firm produces and supplies a good product that is in high demand. Malden Mills products fulfilled a substantial need in winter sports apparel industry. It is easier to be ethical when the top administrators become role models for their ethical and socially responsible behavior. After all, the boss casts a long shadow on the company. (Baumhart, 1968) Feuerstein's shadow fell upon all his employees, from the executives down to the maintenance people.

In the last few years, the practice of downsizing companies has become common, especially in consolidations involving mergers and acquisitions. The September 11, 2001, terrorist destruction in New York and Washington, D.C., has had substantial negative effects on airline travel, hotel occupancy, dining facilities, and entertainment venues. It also reduced the viability of contracts of airlines with their manufacturers. Teal (1996, p.202) quoted Feuerstein in 1996 that he did not reject all downsizing of corporations: "Legitimate downsizing as the result of technological advances or as a result of good industrial engineering? Absolutely, I'm in favor of it. And we do it here all day long." But Feuerstein downsized in such a way that it, too, exemplifies Transforming Justice: "We try to do it in such a way as to minimize human suffering, but the downsizing must be done." (Teal, 1996, p.202) This is an application of an ethical plant closing or employee termination that stresses just cause, due process and mitigation of harmful effects. (McMahon, 1996) Feuerstein told author Thomas Teal in a *Fortune* (1996, p.202) article: "The trick...is to keep growing fast enough to give new jobs to the people technology replaces, to weed out unnecessary jobs without crushing the spirit of the work force."

Malden Mills has also had its share of adversity. In 1981, Feuerstein filed for Chapter 11 protection when it made a failed entry into the fake-fur market. However, its popular Polartec insulation material for outdoor sportswear became so popular that demand for this product literally turned the company around. The fire of 1995 has had some lingering negative effects on the Malden Mills recovery. In 2001, Feuerstein filed for reorganization under Chapter 11 U.S. Bankruptcy Code. In spite of a declared recession, lenders provided $20 million, in addition to the $300 million insurance money. Nonetheless, the company is still $140 million in debt, as of year 2002. The loan allowed Malden Mills to operate during the reorganization. The high cost of servicing the bank debt, a sluggish retail market (especially after September 11, 2001), high construction costs for replacing old buildings, including building a new Polartec plant, and the closing of its upholstery division coalesced to require reorganization under Chapter 11. Critics might suggest that the $25 million commitment to employees in 1995 contributed to the bankruptcy. There is no evidence that this is true. It seems more probable that the high construction cost of building the new Polartec plant might have affected the need to reorganize. Regardless, Feuerstein believes that Malden Mills will emerge as a stronger, more highly focused and profitable company after the reorganization. Babson College business professor Seiders (2002, p.12) stated: "My intuition is that he will remain in a leadership role, but his role will be largely symbolic. He will not be responsible for the key operating and financial decisions."

The Malden Mills case does not easily fall into any of the generally accepted categories or species of justice. It could be argued that it exemplified distributive justice; that is, to give the "goods," whether material or otherwise (like education) from the many to the ones in need. However, Rawls (1971) limits distributive justice to governmental institutions that have legal authority. For him, only the government has the power to bring about change for those who need it. According to this theory, distributive justice is the sharing of the *many* (society in general represented by the government) with the *few* (those in some need). On the contrary, Feuerstein, as an individual not restricted by government regulations, generously shared his wealth with his employees. But it was not the *many* giving to the *few* of traditional distributive justice. He distributed his private wealth to his employees. It was really the *one* (Feuerstein) to the *many* (his employees). This is a different concept of distributive justice. It is also the underpinning of a unique form of Transforming Justice.

CHAPTER 3

Components of
Transforming Justice

Chapter 3 has three principal sections. Each section investigates in depth one component of Transforming Justice in an in-depth study. First, rights are explored. Secondly, the concept and practice of power is examined. Thirdly, past and contemporary theories of justice are reviewed and evaluated in terms of Transforming Justice. Each section examines definitions, methods of acquisition and the exercise of the concept in terms of the previously detailed Profiled Leaders. The specific application of each concept to each Profiled Leader is referenced with respect to each component.

The three components of Transforming Justice have three aspects in common. First of all, each relates to "others"; that is, each component is relational. Secondly, each is perceived as "good" and each is approved by society as such. Thirdly, each is "obligatory." "Obligatory" may be understood—but not necessarily—that rights, power and justice are concepts generally approved of and encouraged by society and require punishment for infractions. "Obligatory" generally, but not exclusively, is associated with ethical and moral standards. This especially applies to the notion of rights. However, the obligation of law may also be included in the concept of Transforming Justice.

Rights are intrinsically related, either ethically, legally or both, to the claims of another. (By law, corporations and independent firms as legal persons share most, but not all, of the rights articulated in the U.S. Bill of Rights.) An individual or group may be either a giver or a receiver of rights. The government and employers are givers of rights. Most citizens and employees are recipients. The "otherness" in the relationship to rights is significant in the discussion. This is apparent in all the Profiled Leaders. Rights are also perceived as a "good." Rights add quality to a person. They even "qualify" a person. They "inform" (that is, add stature) to a person. They imbue a person with a specific quality. For example, a right to the First Amendment freedom of speech permitted Rosa Parks to become the occasion for a boycott of the city bus system that required, by Alabama law, segregated seating.

Power also requires "otherness" and is thus relational. Power may allow its holder to exert control over others. Power is not, strictly speaking, related to the person holding it, as, for example, the power to overcome personal, anti-social tendencies, such as drug abuse. Power will be treated in terms of particular circumstances, but each of these will be related to the "otherness" of the recipient of power. Power is ethically neutral in theory. However, in practice power can only be evaluated based upon in its actual use or abuse. For Americans, the violence perpetrated by terrorists on September 11, 2001 can be seen as an abusive use of power, notably when aggression and retaliation are wrought against innocent people who are not politically involved. The Profiled Leaders illustrate the use of power for good.

In its most basic conceptualization, justice seeks equality as its objective. It is a good by which the rights of all are respected. A person can only have equality within a social context. The "others" might be a person, a group, a corporation, a region or a nation. The measure of a person's equality is always in relation to others. For example, Judge Frank Johnson and Dr. Martin Luther King, Jr. sought equality for others, rather than for themselves. Since Transforming Justice is defined as rights plus power equal justice, of its very nature it is a "good" that relates to others, since rights and power are other-directed.

Besides "otherness" and "good," rights, power and justice must be accepted and approved by society. At this writing, President George W. Bush has an overwhelming approval for his military strategy enacting a war on terrorism. But this approval from the majority in U.S. society is open to multiple interpretations as to what or should be approved by society. Pacifist demonstrators, although comprising a minority of the U.S. population, are contesting the bombing of enemies of the United States. They are proponents of "nonviolence," a common approach of those profiled. The Profiled Leaders illustrate that what the majority of U.S. society approves or disapproves can change, but that such changes are slow. As illustrated previously, textile industry executives criticized Feuerstein's decision to protect his employees from financial disaster. They encouraged him to receive the insurance money and retire, or at least move to a Southern state that had right-to-work laws. His decision fulfilled the three conditions for Transforming Justice of "otherness," ethical or moral "goodness," and a standard that the broader society approves as "obligatory." These components of Transforming Justice are exemplified in all of the Profiled Leaders by examining rights, power and justice in further depth.

RIGHTS

Justice is something that comes second; right comes before justice.
Josef Pieper

The term *right* (unless specifically stated otherwise) means a claim for or against another entity, whether human or corporate. (Garrett, 1986) In terms of this book, it should be understood as a *moral claim*. (Rowan, 2000) A right as a moral claim is not as widely accepted as the conceptualization of a right as a legal claim. For example, the laws of the United States originally permitted slavery and legally treated slaves as chattel or property, not as humans with a moral claim to respect their rights as humans. As such, slaves were property to be bought and sold as cattle. (This matter will also be covered in the section on justice.) The Profiled Leaders convincingly demonstrate that civil law does not always respect the inherent rights of humans. A claim is a particular kind of right that includes the obligation of others to respect this claim. For example, a person's right to private property is to be understood as a duty on the part of others not to steal, use or abuse what belongs to that person. Ozar (1986, p.5) states that "[w]hen we say that someone has a right, our words imply that the moral considerations that are the basis of this statement are more important than any other kinds of moral considerations that might be relevant to the situation." Thus, a right is of the highest order.

Relationship

The focus of a right is a relationship; it is not an object. As a relationship, a right interconnects with another entity, whether human or corporate. A right is a real relationship and not merely a logical or analogous one. The "other" or social context is essential to the concept of this moral claim or a right. (The other components of Transforming Justice, power and justice, are also relational.) Others are morally, not necessarily legally, obligated to respect my rights, as I am morally required to acknowledge and to honor their rights. Claims and moral rights are thus mutually binding. (Gewirth, 1997) As such, moral rights or claims go beyond the unilateral dimension of a promise or other similar commitments.

Rights as Claims

According to Werhane (1985, p.6), "[b]asic moral rights derive from those qualities that uniquely characterize human beings, and in a more restrictive context, rational adults." For all persons to have human rights means that there are conclusive moral reasons that justify the claims. As such, every person can justifiably claim or demand specific rights from all other human beings. (Gewirth, 1987) A human right is a personally oriented, normatively necessary moral requirement. (Gewirth, 1983)

A right informs or qualifies a person. It is a "value added" to the person. In a very loose manner, a right makes a person "more valuable" insofar as the person now has a claim against others in a particular arena. In a sense, a right changes the moral "shape" of the person. A right is usually thought of as a dichotomous construct that may also be categorized as qualitative. It is either present or absent. This is in opposition to the concept of proportion.

Even in quality control, the manufacturing of a product that is 97% defect free is a relative perception. It is not a measurement that is made with a ruler. It is rather an agreement that "perfection" is obtained through "zero" defects but 3% will be an acceptable level. This has been a problem with the threat and analysis of Anthrax in U. S. society: most Americans in this scenario fear physical abuse and medical insufficiency rather than understand infinitesimally low probability of actual exposure and infection, in effect an impossibility to most Americans.

Unlike probability or proportion, a right cannot be measured as greater or lesser as a quantity can. Either a person has a right or does not have it; there is no in between. For example, a person in a democracy has a right to vote or does not have this right, as Susan B. Anthony's crusade highlighted. But a person may *exercise* that right in a lesser or greater degree. For example, in any specific election a citizen may reject the Democratic or the Republican candidate and opt to write in an independent choice. A voter may also decide that it is impossible to determine which candidates to select by reason of the numerous choices. In some counties and states, the voter is presented with a ballot that has more than 100 judges to select. Even with the use of newspapers, legal and government "watch dog" agencies or other pre-voting selection devices, the voter frequently has to depend upon "gut feelings" and general impressions to make these important choices—not a very efficient way to run a democracy! It is thus important to distinguish the *existence* of a right from the *exercise* of a right. As another example of this distinction, a plaintiff or defendant in a court case has a right to a jury trial. She or he might be willing to settle or "plea bargain" rather than exercise this right.

Source of Rights

One conceptualization of the source of rights is, that human rights are inborn. Just the fact of existence is sufficient to establish such basic rights, such as the right to life, the right to own property, the right to face one's accuser, and similar basic rights. This has traditionally been called the natural rights theory. More contemporary ethicists prefer the concept of a moral rights theory rather than a natural rights theory. This theory will be developed at length in the section on justice, with specific reference to the Profiled Leaders.

An alternative explanation is that the source of rights comes from society: everyone is entitled to receive those rights that society grants, or ought to grant. When society refuses to acknowledge something as a claim, such as the right to life in all its forms from conception to the death, it cannot *be* a claim and, therefore, it cannot be a right. Society, not necessarily the government, determines these rights. This is labeled the social good theory of rights. The

Profiled Leaders illustrate that members of a society may, and probably should, challenge the civil laws that restrict human or moral rights. Social good theory is based on the proposition of providing the greatest good for the greatest number, a vestige of utilitarianism. This theory is the backbone of a democracy. In America, society has moved from racial segregation to racial desegregation to racial integration. The change has been slow but historically obvious. It took society many decades to acknowledge that the human rights of minorities should be legal rights as well.

A third explanation of the source of rights articulates that the only rights a person has are those that positive law establishes or grants. In this conceptualization the law, whether civil or church (canonical), is supreme. Positive law becomes the source and origin of all human rights. It denies in essence the human rights postulated by the natural law theory. It also rejects the social good theory of the greatest good for the greatest number. Only rights that the positive law grants are acknowledged and respected. If a right is not granted by civil law, it does not exist. Even human rights depend upon the mandates of positive law. This position is called the positive law theory. These differences will be treated more thoroughly in the section on justice.

All three theoretical conceptualizations acknowledge that rights are essential to justice, although the origins and roles of these rights differ. However, none of these theories as such links rights to power. For each, rights are not dependent upon power and are, in fact, disassociated with it. Only Transforming Justice incorporates power as intrinsic to the realization of rights. As stated as the major premise of this book, power, as well as rights, is required for the conceptualization of Transforming Justice.

Acquiring Rights

In order to have and to exercise Transforming Justice, a person, whether human or legally considered person (such as a corporation), has to acquire rights. (In the Dartmouth College case of 1816, the U.S. Supreme Court, under Chief Justice John Marshall, decided that corporations are considered legally to be persons.) However, the acquisition of rights is dependent upon a person's theoretical view of rights. Natural law, social good or positive law. All bestowed differently defined rights. Transforming Justice subscribes to the natural right theory. According to the natural rights or moral rights theory, many—not all—rights come from the fact of a person's existence as a human being. These rights may be claims of the disabled, the dispossessed, the poor, the unemployed, and the homeless. The powerful, the wealthy, the educated, the property owners and the stockholders, also have claims. However, the latter are generally protected and reinforced by strong legislation. In addition, they have powerful resources to provide the best legal advocates. One might question how the legal disputes of large corporations such as Microsoft would be resolved if they were represented by a court appointed lawyer, as are many of the poor and the powerless.

The U.S. *Declaration of Independence* refers to basic inalienable rights that accrue to all citizens. The roots of these rights flow from the natural law perspective. In order to attain Transforming Justice, a person must first acquire rights: rights come before justice. Indeed, rights are the "material" of justice: without rights, justice in any of its species has nothing to equalize. No matter which of the theories of rights mentioned above to which a person subscribes, he or she may acquire rights through a variety of means. As stated above, the natural rights theory grants human rights to every person. The Profiled Leaders were not only aware of their rights, but also exercised their power to make these rights operative. Among those profiled, Cesar Chavez seemed to be an obvious proponent of basic human rights from the perspective of his nitty-gritty everyday experience. Like the other Profiled Leaders, he went beyond the theoretical to the practical through the use of his uniquely powerful experiences.

Contracts and Rights

In addition to being born with rights, there are additional ways to acquire rights. The most obvious is through contracts. When a person buys property, she or he acquires the right to use, to lend, to sell and in some circumstances even to abuse the property, according to natural law, civil law or social standards. A person can also inherit rights, as illustrated by John XXIII with respect to canonical rights and Feuerstein related to property rights. A person or a group of people can also acquire rights through civil legislation and by virtue of authoritative procedures in institutions, such as universities and religious organizations. Rights may also be acquired in a democratic society through legitimate voting procedures. These refer primarily to the rights given to people in positions of civil authority such as the rights of presidents, senators, governors, mayors and other government administrators.

As stated above, rights are oftentimes acquired through contracts. Though there are numerous types of contracts, contracts in this discussion are limited to four different kinds: first, the explicit contract; second, the implicit contract; third, the market model; and fourth, the social market model. (McMahon, 1986) The rationale underlying contract theory is that the title or source of rights can be established only through some form of contract that determines mutually agreeable rights and obligations between the parties. The parties in a contract may have a direct or an indirect claim on each other. Direct claims clearly spell out rights and obligations in a contract, whether oral or written. Indirect claims do not clearly determine rights and obligations of either party. For example, the social responsibility of a firm to a local community is generally not clearly articulated or established. It can differ, related to the amount of social power the firm has or assumes. A company in a single-industry town has more social power than a conglomerate in a large city. (This concept will also be covered more thoroughly in the section on justice.) The exceptions are planned cities, such as Reston, Virginia, and Columbia, Maryland, where specific industries, size of plants, number of retail stores and other factors enter into a direct and explicit contract between the different claimants and the local government.

On the contrary, indirect claimants, such as local communities and competitors, have a serious problem trying to determine and specify the legitimate source of their rights and their obligations to the local society. Plant-closings in a single-industry municipality exemplify this problem. Eells and Walton (1961) touch upon this concern when they state that the referents in these ambiguous terms are unclear in determining rights and obligations.

Explicit Contracts

Any explicit contract in one that lends itself to a one-on-one relationship with the "other." It might be understood as a form of exchange justice and takes place between two parties. The details are spelled out frequently in specific legal terms, either orally or in writing. More often than not, it is mutually acceptable: you do this and I will do that; you respect my rights and I will fulfill my obligation to you. Feuerstein in his commitment to continue to pay the salaries of the employees, to maintain their health insurance and to grant a bonus was indeed creating and honoring an explicit contract. It was more than a unilateral promise. It was a mutual agreement. This was an explicit contract between employer and employee: the employer was willing to pay these costs; the employee was granted the right to expect them. The employee could have rejected the offer. As the employer, he had no legal obligation to the employee beyond that stipulated in the union contract which was negotiated before the factory fire. The employee had no *legal* obligation to accept this generous offer. The employer might still have a *moral* obligation to assist these employees in some way. Keith Davis's *mandatum* that the greater the social power, the greater the social obligation applies in the Malden Mills case. Feuerstein had both social power and economic power in Lawrence, Massachusetts. He fulfilled his commitment to his employees and to the local community. Pieper (1965, p.49) believes that "[b]y reason of something he has done, something is now due to him....Now this act of giving is an act of justice, and it has as its condition, then, the fact that something is due to his neighbor." The relationship between employer and employee at Malden Mills was one in which each interacted with respect to each other's rights. This is an optimum illustration of the application of contract theory. Feuerstein acquired both his rights and his basic power through inheritance. But he also believed that he, as the CEO of the company, should have sensitivity to the human equation. (Seeger, 2001) This sensitivity was communicated to him from his grandfather, his father and his religious beliefs, as stated in his profile.

Like all specific contracts, the firm-local agreement in a planned community establishes a relationship that allows no change except through renegotiations and tends to forestall any dynamism that stimulates growth and quality-of-life within a community. The price of security seems to override other values, such as growth and development. Furthermore, planned communities also tend to limit corporate social responsibility beyond what is mandatory by contract. This type of contract also limits a company's social responsiveness to a changing environment.

The rights and obligations that arise from the contractual agreement in planned communities should not be confused with the negotiations over site, tax breaks, and land development that local communities may grant to business firms and others. Such incentives are unilateral proposals that are used to obtain a commitment to move into the community. The administrators of the City of Chicago and of the State of Illinois provided a generous package of benefits to Boeing when the company announced that it was planning to move its headquarters to a more central location in the year 2000. Chicago was chosen (essentially "won") over Denver and Dallas. Although explicit and negotiated to a degree, these enticements are granted privileges, rather than rights and obligations.

Implied Contracts

A second type of contract is the implied contract. The basis for this so-called contract is a continuous and prolonged interaction between a firm and a local community. Single-industry municipalities, such as Neodesha, Kansas (a former refinery home of Amoco) and Kenosha, Wisconsin (a former assembly plant of Chrysler Corporation) believe that there is a contract of mutual rights and obligations that develops over time in such co-dependent relationships. Again, the Malden Mills case mentioned in the profiles is related to what Garrett (1966, p.47) states:

> Quite aside from legal provisions...there are implicit contracts which limit or modify the right of both employer and employee...Regardless of explicit contractual provisions, both employer and employee have obligations to each other which arise first from their common humanity and secondly from the definite social situation in which the agreement was made. This means that each side must take into consideration the legitimate interests and expectations of the other side. While such interests may not be decisive, they must be considered lest one be indifferent to the good of another human being.

In addition, Garrett (1986, p.72) refers to the implicit contract between employer and employee that places an obligation on the employer "...to keep secret a great deal of information about the employee" and to limit its use, such as health reports, psychological and psychiatric tests and other personal information. Garrett (1966, p.185) provides a third perspective on the implicit contract:

Because of this (mutual need between a firm and a local community) continued association gives rise to a real, though vague and implied contract. Business normally expects that the local community will maintain a reasonable and orderly tax policy and encourage good labor relations. The community, on its side, assumes that business will strive to maintain stable employment patterns as well as pay taxes and protect community resources. Although the contract between the firm and the community is not enforceable by law, it generates a real obligation on both sides, since orderly social life and community development are impossible without it.

Garrett does acknowledge in his 1986 second edition that law court decisions have shown that implied contracts might exist in some unjust dismissals that were against public policy, as well as in some statements of commitment found in company personnel manuals.

Implied contracts may bring about a twofold problem. First, an implied contract is usually compared to an explicit contract; that is, the rights and obligations of an implied contract *flow* from an explicit contract. For example, company policy related to specifics of expense accounts flows from the explicit contract to work for a firm in accordance with its legitimate policies and practices. In stipulating rights and obligations between a firm and a local community that the theory of implied contract proposes, these mutual rights and obligations do not derive from an express contract (unless expressly agreed upon, as stated above.) Feuerstein's explicit commitment to his employees only indirectly affected the city of Lawrence; this does not appear to fulfill the requirements of an implied contract of a firm to a local community. Secondly, the source of mutual rights and obligations in an implied contract that Garrett (1966) proposes arise from the expectations and assumptions of each contracting party. Susan B. Anthony believed that the United States government had an implicit contract flowing from the Constitution to grant as many civil rights to women as it does to men. Expectations are generally the result of desires and hopes. On the contrary, assumptions are frequently a form of substitutions for facts that cannot be verified under current circumstances; nonetheless, the person, in making assumptions, acts in a manner that he or she considers to be reasonable. Both expectations and assumptions are subjective. They thus become "as if" operating norms.

But assumptions and expectations are not the source of rights. An expectation may become a source of rights when it is based on a pre-established criterion. For example, an MBA student expects to get a high grade in a course if she or he fulfills the conditions detailed in the class syllabus. This is a conditional contract: *if* a student fulfills the requirements listed in the syllabus, he or she will receive a high grade. A conditional contract becomes ethically and legally binding when the *condition* (or contingency) is fulfilled. Susan B. Anthony's expectations were not fulfilled even after passing the Amendment that assured woman suffrage; she expected that all civil rights would be granted to women if they were able to vote.

Market Contract Model

The market contract model of classical economics is a third source of rights. It is essentially a buyer-seller contract within a free competitive environment: a seller sells at the highest obtainable price and the buyer buys at the lowest possible price. Size, economic power and other factors theoretically need not affect this relationship, which is also an explicit contract when the terms are mutually agreeable. The market contract model as such does not cover the means employed to arrive at these terms like power, supply, demand or environment. The market contract model thus sidesteps a major factor in any contract: the relative size, power and impact of the contracting parties on each other and on society. Cesar Chavez assumed that once he had the political support of the farm workers in his union, he would be empowered to work toward changing the plight of migrant workers through legislation in the state of California. Apparently, he did not foresee the market power of the Teamsters Union to attract his union members with a more attractive contract.

As a legal person with rights, privileges and obligations derived from the corporate charter, a firm has no more legal obligations to a local community than any other citizen, according to classical economists such as Milton Friedman (1962). Thus, a buyer-seller relationship is strictly external; it has no intrinsic effect on the institution. Consequently, the local community becomes nothing more than a legal environment in which to do business.

Feuerstein's decisions totally reject the tenets and practices of the market contract model, as his decisions in the Malden Mills case exemplify. He strongly believed in respecting the human rights of his employees and contributed greatly to the local community before and after the fire. (Seeger, 2001) But he also believed that producing quality products in a favorable environment would become profitable.

Social Contract Theory

The final contract model is called the social contract theory. This theory has become popular in the realm of business ethics since the 1980s in determining moral standards for the interaction of companies and society. Locke, Hobbes and Rousseau proposed the social contract theory with respect to those who govern and to those who are governed. Carroll (1996, p.20) writes that "[t]he social contract is a set of two-way understandings that characterize the relationship between major institutions....The social contract is changing, and this change is a direct outgrowth of the increased importance of the social environment." Nonetheless, the social contract theory must resolve certain core issues: 1) why it would be rational for everyone to agree on its terms; 2) the use of outside devices such as Rawls' (1971) "the veil of ignorance" as part of the theory; 3) why individuals would be willing to act according to the terms of the contract; and, 4) the demonstration that this social contract is realistic and based on human nature. (Dunfee, 1999) The theory contains two different types of social contracts: a hypothetical social contract and the actual existing social contracts in communities. (Dunfee, 1999) The first is theoretical; the second is practical. The most widely acknowledged hypothetical is Rawls' "veil of ignorance" to effect objectivity. This refers to a context in which all the participants of the social contract come together without prejudice, preconceived notions and anything else that would affect the objectivity of the social contract. Specific ethical obligations and rights are deduced from this theoretical contract. Nonetheless, according to Dunfee (1999), the ultimate and definitive source of norms must be the attitudes and behaviors of the members of the relevant communities. Donaldson (1982) and Donaldson /Dunfee (1995, 1994) have thoroughly discussed social contract theory and have offered their own interpretation. Subsequently they have further developed their Integrative Social Contracts Theory (ISCT) in a 1999 publication of *Ties That Bind: A Social Contracts Approach to Business Ethics*. (*Business and Society Review* has devoted a special issue on the different reactions to this book [Vol. 105, No. 4, Winter, 2000].)

Perhaps Cesar Chavez more than any of the other Profiled Leaders, even Feuerstein, illustrates the strengths and weaknesses of this theory. Three factors of the social contract theory apply: first, the theoretical base; secondly, the deductive rights and obligations; and, thirdly, the definitive source of the norms that are based on the attitudes of the community. The theoretical base for Chavez was the right to work under humane conditions. Chavez frequently referenced the social teachings of the Catholic Church, especially the papal encyclicals (authoritative teachings) on the rights and obligations of employees and employers. (Cima, 2001) Chavez deduced from these teachings that California law prohibiting the unionization of migrants and the political power of the farmers were at least unethical, if not contrary to the U.S. Constitution and Bill of Rights. If "relevant communities" are the definitive *source* for norms (Dunfee, 1999), the source excluded the migrant farm workers. The migrant workers were definitely "relevant" to the success of the farmers, who owned the property and its yield. But somehow they were not perceived as "relevant" members of the agriculture industry (the "community" in this situation) in terms of rights, and as such the right to unionize.

Another perspective of the social contract theory is that it is always changing. (Carroll, 1996) The environment is one in which the parties of a contract can become more hostile or more favorable; it rarely stays the same. Chavez experienced this dynamic contextual change as he increased the base of his economic, social and political power. The agreement among the participants shifted from total rejection of his goals, methods and means toward a tolerated acceptance. Gandhi, King and Mandela went through similar progressions in their journeys towards equality.

Means of Acquiring Rights

The four social contract theories illustrate both the underlying rationale and the acquisition of rights through contracts. It is now possible to examine briefly the most commonly used means that the Profiled Leaders employed in exercising their rights: boycotts, marches, and civil disobedience to unjust laws. These methods will be treated more completely in the Observations section in Chapter 4. It is sufficient to recall that these behaviors were exercised in seeking the goal of equality. Anthony, Gandhi, King, Chavez and Mandela employed all of these methods.   John XXIII apparently employed civil disobedience in protecting Jewish immigrants. The exceptions were Johnson as a federal judge and Feuerstein as a considerate employer who had no need to employ any of these means to exercise their rights.

In conclusion, the Profiled Leaders provided historical examples for understanding the concept, acquisition and exercise of rights in contemporary society. No matter which theory is chosen for adherent belief, rights are always relational and, therefore, social, and they precede justice.

POWER

The purpose of power is to realize justice.
Joseph Pieper

Psychologists, social scientists, social workers, legal scholars, political theorists, economists, ethicists and moral theologians, perceive, investigate and evaluate power in different ways.   Some see power from a negative viewpoint as a form of coercion; it can be used to further the interests of a person or institution at the expense of others.   Others see power as a liberating force; power is frequently a condition for obtaining civil rights, as the profiles testify. Some see it neither as coercion nor liberation, but rather as a neutral factor in decision-making. Marxists see power as a conflict of social classes that requires governmental control. It may be said that no single definition of power covers its many forms and aspects. (Lukes, 1986) It is not the purpose of this book to compare or evaluate the different theories of power. Rather, the focus is to elucidate how power is applied to Transforming Justice.

Americans tend to have a negative view of power. Years ago, Kotter (1977, p. 125) wrote: "Americans, as a rule, are not generally very comfortable with power or its dynamics. We often distrust and question the motives of people who we think actively seek power... .The overall attitude and feeling towards power... is negative." The Selekmans (1961, p.13) expand this view when they wrote: "We are haunted by the age-old suspicion that power is evil, as indeed it is, unless it is checked, contained, and directed." The September 11, 2001 terrorist attacks on New York City and Washington, D.C. confirm this negative view. This is not a new conceptualization. In 1971, when I taught a summer school course on power at St. Mary's of California, a nun responded by saying, "That dirty topic!" I reminded her that as a teacher and a religious she had power over her pupils. It shocked her. When the School of Business Administration of the University of Virginia sponsored a workshop on the ethical use of power in business, the President of General Motors Canada stated that he did not feel that he exercised power in his decisions. As he gave his speech, I said to myself: "Did he ever ask his employees if they felt the brunt of his power!" As is evident, the powerful are not always aware of their control and impact on the lives of others. Happily, some are. A friend gave me a needlepoint pillow on which was embroidered "To Teach Is To Touch A Life Forever," as a reminder that teaching is a powerful tool. Power can be used for both good and evil. Power can be used to bring harm on others, as the terrorist schools in the Middle East and the Pacific Rim countries have clearly demonstrated.

From the opposite perspective, it is the powerless who are actually conscious of their lack of power. An analogous use of the concept of power can be developed by examining what being powerless means. Power or powerlessness is truly in the perception of the beholder. If others perceive a person as powerful, that person becomes powerful, at least in the eyes of the person who is in a dependent position. Conversely, a powerful person becomes so with the possession of resources that make others dependent. As an example, I was given a position of authority in a small school. The students were not informed of this appointment. When the students needed help or permission to begin or complete a project, they went to another teacher. This other teacher graciously granted the students requests, and thus assumed power. The students ultimately deduced from these actions that the other teacher was in charge and thus responded to this power. Most of the Profiled Leaders were perceived at first by government officials as people without power—which in reality was the case. As the men and women gradually obtained power, the perception changed. Society and governments had to recognize the shift in power.

Held (1997, p.494) expresses his negative assessment of power and powerlessness: "One important conception sees it [power] as paradigmatically a capacity to cause others to do what they would otherwise not do." For example, the vast majority of Moslems in the world reject the terrorist movement as contrary to the basic tenets of their religion. Yet, terrorist violence in the United States and other countries has been proclaimed by a faction of Moslems to be a "Jihad" or "holy war." In another example in the United States, extremists from the "pro-life" persuasion consider killing abortionists and destroying their property as a morally good act. There is similarity between these examples in content, if not in context. As was seen in the profiles, it is one thing to demonstrate against unjust laws; it is quite another to inflict or to suffer violence. Violent actions can emanate from threat, force, domination or some other form of power over others to do something they would ordinarily not do. The threat of losing a job in corporate mergers is real and can be exemplified in such consolidations as the British Petroleum/Amoco and the Mercedes Benz/Chrysler mergers. Both of these merging corporations were purported to be equal partners in the newly formed company, but in fact, both British Petroleum and Mercedes Benz became dominant at the executive and managerial levels. Job loss became a greater threat and a sad reality for Amoco and Chrysler employees in the United States.

Energy and Power

The most basic perception of power is energy. Energy moves people, animals and even objects such as machines, computers and automobiles. The energy for moving people is different from the energy of animals seeking their prey; it also differs from electrical energy that is required to move electric motors and computers, and from the energy required to heat houses and to move automobiles. With the exception of the energy of animals, which is innate, the other forms of energy need direction—human direction—to operate. The electric light needs a switch for direction to be turned on or off; pull the wrong switch and the electricity goes on in another direction. The computer needs constant instruction to produce specific results whether it be word-processing, financial calculations, or printing an original greeting card. Natural gas to heat houses requires an input source, a furnace and a thermostat for control. Automobiles need ignition and gasoline to start and steering for direction. Guardini (1961, p.1) clearly distinguishes the difference between energy and power: "Energy becomes power only when some consciousness recognizes it, some will capable of decision directs it towards specific goals." To become power, such energy needs human direction.

Definition of Power

Power in Transforming Justice may be defined *as the capacity to effect change in others according to the intent of the agent.* Capacity is capability or ability; it is not volume, space or accommodation as it is in engineering or in architecture. Effecting or bringing about change is essential to the concept of Transforming Justice. It does not involve a change in substance, it is rather the sense of changing shape, as stated earlier. Changing is synonymous with transforming. The power to change is quantitative; it is usually measured by its effect or impact. As quantitative, it may also be added to or subtracted from, as every politician is aware on polling day. In the profiles, the effects of the use of power were obvious: changes were wrought in governments, changes took the form of relevant legislation, changes took place as church reform and changes effected economic stability.

Like rights and justice, power is relational. It always affects others, depending upon the form of power that is used, over whom it is exercised, and how it is applied. This became all too apparent in the United States on and since September 11, 2001. The political relationship between the U.S. and other world powers was clarified and made overt. Each of the Profiled Leaders exhibits some form of direct relationship to others. The direction of her or his unique power manifested itself in pursuing objectives and ultimate goals.

There are several different ways of perceiving power. Epstein (1973) proposes four levels of corporate power: macro (related to the business system in general), intermediate level (involving several firms in the same industry), micro level (referring to a single firm in an industry) and individual level (a single executive within a company). Carroll (1996) proposes six spheres in which power resides; namely, economic, social/cultural, individual, technological, environmental, and political. The Selekmans (1956) propose four kinds of power: science/technology, business, government, and moral. Each of these approaches has merit in determining contexts in which power can reside. For the purpose of analyzing Transforming Justice, four categories will be examined: economic, political, social and moral.

Power may also be viewed as interactive, or, perhaps more accurately, as transferable. Power is not static; after all, power is energy. It can empower other categories. Thus, for example, political power can generate economic or social power; moral power may influence political power. A concern in the United States is that wealthy candidates for political office can afford to advertise more frequently and more strategically, positively and negatively, to convince potential voters that their positions are admirable and that their opponents are not qualified by reason of inadequate performance, questionable personal behavior or suitability for the position. The biographies of the Profiled Leaders illustrate this interaction of power: the moral power of Gandhi, the nonviolent social power of King, and the moral power of Chavez affected the political power of the governments with which they interacted.

In the strict sense of the word, a person does not have power over himself or herself. In the broader sense, a person does have power over her or his actions, such as the personal strength or power to overcome the problem of alcohol or drug addition. But even in these situations, outside help is usually necessary, such as affiliation with Alcoholics Anonymous or other counseling. It appears that all power, even the moral power of Gandhi, comes from the outside of the powerful person. The tenets of Hinduism, the Muslim Quoran, the scriptures of the Hebrew Old Testament and the Christian New Testament deeply influenced Gandhi's, and in turn Chavez's, approach to finding Truth.

The intent of the agent is so important that power cannot exist without some type of direction from the possessor of power. Guardini (1961, p.4) goes so far that he writes that "[P]ower receives its character only when someone becomes aware of it, determines its use, and puts it to work." He then adds an ethical dimension of accountability once the person is empowered by stating that "[T]his means that someone must answer for it."

Source of Power

The source of power, unlike the grounds for rights, is less certain. Depending upon the kind of power, it may be obtained through inheritance, contract, force, competition, manipulation or fraud. (McMahon, 1999) Not all of these sources, under certain circumstances, are morally justified. Transforming

Justice as defined here, however, is always morally acceptable. By definition (rights plus power equals justice), rights not only come before justice, but power also precedes justice. Legitimate rights are ethically good by their nature, as seen in the natural right theory and the natural law. (See the following section on justice for an in-depth discussion.) On the contrary, power is ethically neutral in and of itself, but becomes ethically good or bad when it becomes part of a human act. Moreover, in any concrete decision or application power is no longer neutral, but depends upon the good or evil intention of the power holder. From the viewpoint of the United States and her allies, terrorism is assessed to be an evil use of power. Aquinas (S.T., II-II, q.2, a.4, ad. 2) writes: "...that power is towards good and evil." The definition of Transforming Justice, as it does rights, places power before justice.   But it also places power chronologically after rights. This interest in location and time is not without merit. In essence it guarantees that power must not be used to obtain or to justify rights. In effect, this order states that "might does not make right" in any of the senses of rights that have previously been described. But power can be used in *exercising* rights; indeed, without some type of power rights cannot be effectively exercised. The notion of Transforming Justice suggests that power can be a legitimate means to exercise those rights that have been causally obtained, or made claim to, through some ethical source or title, such as natural law. All the theories described above and all the Profiled Leaders employed power to make preexisting rights operative. Only Transforming Justice, as distinct from other theories of justice, incorporates power as an intrinsic component of justice. (The agents of distributive justice generally use the power of the state to bring about proportional equality, as will be considered later.)

There are six means of acquiring power. These means are not mutually exclusive. One form of power (such as legal power) could lead to or incorporate another kind of power (such as social), as in the profile of Johnson (legal) and King (social). Two assumptions accompany these six means of power. The first assumption is that the six means of acquiring power need not be mutually exclusive; it is possible to inherit property (economic power), but to require the force of the courts to obtain it (legal power). This did not apply to Feuerstein; he did not have to go to court to inherit the Malden Mills. The second assumption might legitimately be challenged. It is that individuals are not entirely powerless in any situation. For example, Mandela was not entirely powerless when he was in prison on Robbin Island; he educated other prisoners, assisted jail guards with their legal problems and was able to communicate secretly with followers outside the prison walls. Thus, although people might be physically helpless against brute force or other types of physical or psychological power, they can sometimes still retain their moral power. Such was the case with many Jews during the Nazi holocaust.

The first means of acquiring power is inheritance. It may be viewed as a "given" power. It does not in itself include the notion of earning or merit or any form of a right except inheritance. Inherited power can come in monarchical succession (such as that given to a king or a queen, as in Great Britain), family wealth (as exemplified in the Kennedy and Rockefeller families), or in organizational succession (such as when a successor is hand-picked to become the next president of a company, as happens frequently in family-owned businesses). In the profiled examples, Feuerstein inherited power associated both with wealth and the family business started by his grandfather.

The second way to obtain power is through authority. Authority is a granted power. Sometimes it is legally granted through appointment, as is the case of the U.S. Supreme Court justices. John XXIII was granted papal authority through the votes of cardinals in the consistory or church council, which is called to succeed a deceased pope. Judge Frank Johnson was granted authority in federal courts through an appointment; it was not through an election, as in some local judgeships. His appointment had to be approved by Congress. Sometimes it is said that a person "speaks with authority." This is a perceived power; it is not a granted power. It is a power that is recognized by others, whether a person's peers, colleagues, competitors or, in some cases the media. Almost everyone considered Walter Cronkite, a highly respected CBS news commentator, as a person who "speaks with authority." Indubitably, he manifested the positive power of the press.

A third way of obtaining power is through contractual agreements that are to the advantage of one party. It can be done abusively by payoffs or simple manipulation. Most of these are applications of the Roman law of *do ut des,* which freely translated means that "I will give you something so that you will perform this or that act." Prostitution falls into this category. In general, however, in order to be morally justified, power must be obtained through legitimate contracts between consenting parties who do not unduly or manipulatively take advantage of any party to the contract. Chavez obtained legally recognized power when he signed the contracts between the United Farm Workers and the farm owners. Feuerstein empowered his employees when he stated that he would provide financial aid to them.

A fourth way of obtaining power is through competition. Power that is gained or obtained through morally acceptable competition is justifiably earned and deserved in a capitalistic society: "To the victor goes the spoils!" Competition is intrinsically necessary in sports, whether it be an elementary school soccer team or individuals and teams in the Olympics. Competition is also endemic to business. When competition is eliminated through some form of agreement among companies in the same industry (for example, through price fixing), it is a use of power that violates the United States antitrust laws. Mergers and acquisitions are another means that corporations employ to obtain more competitive power. It does not seem that many of the Profiled Leaders employed competition in the strict sense to gain power. However, Mandela competed in fighting for a multiracial state while his opponent supported an all-black South Africa. In addition, Chavez competed with the Teamsters for union membership.

The fifth source of obtaining power is manipulation. Shostrom (1967, viii) describes a manipulator as "[A] person who exploits, uses, and/or controls... others as things in certain self-defeating ways." Apart from sociological and psychological dimensions in manipulation, there is the disturbing ethical concern of withholding the truth from the person being manipulated. It also impinges upon the basic human rights of the person manipulated in that she or he is not fully aware of the reality of the situation. Thus, the manipulated person does not act freely and might well be acting against his or her own best interests. Manipulators use persons as objects, as means to bring about their own ends, frequently at the expense of the manipulated. Manipulated power cannot be justified to obtain Transforming Justice. Manipulation is an abuse of power and thus has no place in Transforming Justice. Some might perceive Mandela's clever use of his talents, such as giving legal advice to prison guards, as a form of manipulation. However, he did not act against the freedom of his clients nor did he act against their best interests. Through his legal advice, he gradually gained the trust of the guards. In this and other ways, Mandela slowly developed a power base that ultimately challenged South African apartheid.

The sixth means of obtaining power is through force. Force is raw power. As power, force is also ethically neutral; that is, its moral status depends on how the agent uses force. A person becomes an object of force for some particular reason, such as politics, geographical borders, religion, status, authority, or other factors. For example, Berle (1969, p.413) views force as the ultimate instrument in international power: "Force is still the *Ultima ratio regum*—the final argument of sovereigns." The September 11, 2001 acts of terrorism and reaction to it from the United States and its allies illustrate Berle's position. Force can be perceived in various ways: physical, psychological, economic, legal, social and, most importantly for Transforming Justice, moral power or force. For the purpose of seeing the role of force in Transforming Justice, as illustrated by the Profiled Leaders, it is useful to limit the notion of force to physical force, such as war or capital punishment, and to nonviolent force, such as boycotts, marches and non-cooperation with legal regulations that oppress or suppress human dignity. Even civil disobedience may be considered a type of nonviolent force.

Force as such does have a place in Transforming Justice. It was the nonviolent social force of Dr. Martin Luther King, Jr. and others that created an environment of concern for the injustice of segregation that Congress could not ignore, as it had in the previous century. Congress passed the Civil Rights Act of 1964, which prohibited discrimination on the basis of race, color, religion, sex, or natural origin. It was the legal force of Judge Frank Johnson that permitted King to use nonviolent means to obtain racial equality. Through both legal and moral force, civil rights became a legal mandate and a social base for such applications as affirmative action. Anthony, Gandhi, Chavez, and Mandela used boycotts, marches and non-cooperation, all of which led to civil disobedience, to develop a moral force to bring about change.

Physical force has a different set of rules. Of itself it is ethically neutral, as is all power in the abstract. However, in the concrete it may or may not be a morally legitimate means for obtaining objectives or goals. The use of physical force frequently impinges upon the human dignity or the civil rights of other citizens. Excessive force, which might be used as a means to bring about a good end, is most likely unethical. For example, the saturation bombings of German cities and the use of the atomic bomb in Japan during World War II have been judged by ethicists, moral theologians and others to be an excessive use of physical force. Uninvolved civilians, as well as members of the military, were bombed or murdered. The acts of terrorism and bio-terrorism in the United States on and since September 11, 2001 illustrate excessive use of force. Some Americans, especially pacifists and other protesters, have questioned the ethical dimension of the American bombings in Afghanistan and Iraq. Furthermore, it is not clear who are the actual perpetrators in this war of terrorism. The burden of proof that this use of force is ethically or morally acceptable lies with the perpetrators of physical force. There is no ethical reason that a "holy war" is a just war. The end does not justify the means in Transforming Justice; it is not the greatest good for the greatest number nor does a good end justify questionable or evil means. Aquinas (S.T., II-II, q. 65, a.2, ad 2) makes a distinction between the physical force of a perfect community (civil authority) and that of an imperfect community (family). The first could mean imprisonment or even capital punishment; many contemporary ethicists and moral theologians would disagree with this application. The second legitimate use of physical force in a family, an imperfect society, might be to punish an unruly child, but not to harm the offspring. At first glance a perfect society, that is a duly recognized government, has not officially admitted that it fosters or encourages terrorism. On the other hand, not all the involved states have denounced or denied the use of terrorism. Thus the use of force in the current world situation is unclear in its moral overtones, but nonetheless fraught with divergent views of the sacredness of life and moral perspective in this war-torn environment.

Control

Control is an exercise of power; as such, it is not a means of obtaining power. Control is an application of power, and, as such, it is neutral in theory but can be good or evil in practice. A person can exercise power over others, but not necessarily control them. A teacher has authority over students but need not control their ability to investigate, conceptualize or experiment.

Psychological control is a source of power that has no place in Transforming Justice. This includes drugs, consciously devised for deprivation, exploitation of people, and other activities that prey on the dignity of the person and are exploitive. Similarly, terrorism and bio-terrorism and threats associated with them have no place in Transforming Justice.

By reason of its nature, control might be more pervasive in authority (government), inheritance (limiting conditions), force (war) and manipulation (psychological methods of obtaining personal information). Control may also be exercised through contract, especially in acquisitions and mergers. As stated above, British Petroleum's (BP) acquisition of Amoco was initially announced as "a marriage of equals." The egalitarian marriage did not last long. BP took clear control, causing the top executives of Amoco to "resign" within a relatively short time. As stated previously, persons vested with authority—teachers, religious leaders, business executives, and government officials—are imbued with certain power to control. When a person or a group exceeds the authority of the appointment, higher authority then controls through various means. For example, secular and religious institutions frequently control subordinates through budgets.

Control may ethically exist in Transforming Justice. Feuerstein controlled the future of his employees in a positive manner. Judge Johnson used his legal power to control applications of First Amendment freedoms. In both of these cases, controlled power was imperative to achieve the goal of justice. In the Gandhi and Mandela profiles, power, and ultimately control, shifted from one entity to another. In the case of Gandhi, this shift of control was from the British establishment in India to the popular leader. In the case of Mandela, control moved from the apartheid government in South Africa to his proposed democracy. In each case, control shifted from questionably constituted authority to freely chosen governments.

Berle's Laws of Power

Having reviewed the different dimensions of power in Transforming Justice, it is useful to enumerate what Adolf Berle (1969, p.37) calls "the five natural laws of power." Berle spent his life studying the concept of power beginning with his attendance at the Versailles Peace Conference of 1918-1919. He made his final contribution to the field in his last major publication simply entitled *Power* in 1969. In addition to his teaching at Columbia University and his role as consultant to presidents, most notably to Franklin D. Roosevelt, he wrote ten books on power. He focused a number of his publications on the economic power of business corporation stockholders and the administrative power of corporation executives and managers. Over the course of his theorizing and myriad applications, he developed his five natural laws of power. In his final publication, *Power* (1969), he applies these rules in detail. The five rules are:

One: Power invariably fills any vacuum in human organization. As between chaos and power, the latter always prevails.

Two: Power is invariably personal. There is no such thing as "class power," "elite power," or "group power," though classes, elites, and groups may assist processes of organization by which power is lodged in individuals.

Three: Power is invariably based on a system of ideas or philosophy. Absent such a system or philosophy, the institutions essential to power cease to be reliable, power ceases to be effective, and the power holder is eventually displaced.

Four: Power is exercised through, and depends on, institutions. By their existence, they limit, come to control, and eventually confer or withdraw power.

Five: Power is invariably confronted with, and acts in the presence of, a field of responsibility. The two constantly interact, in hostility or co-operation, in conflict or through some form of dialogue, organized or unorganized, made part of, or perhaps intruding into, the institutions on which power depends.

Berle illustrates each of these laws with copious historical examples, ranging from ancient times to a more recent New York blackout, where motorists followed the direction of a teenager with a flashlight rather than experience the chaos of gridlock caused by non-functioning traffic lights. The German people preferred the dictatorship of Hitler to the chaos of the post World War I Weimar Republic. After September 11, 2001, it appears that most Americans accepted, almost without reservation, the decisions of President George W. Bush to do what he proposed necessary to counteract terrorism. The five laws could be applied to Hitler and to many modern leaders who have ascended to and lost power. It is not the purpose of this book to reiterate Berle's examples. Rather, this book will illustrate how the Profiled Leaders fulfilled these five laws of power. Each of the five laws will be treated separately.

Power and Chaos

Between chaos and power, the latter always prevails. Mandela through his persistent efforts of nonviolence that led to the chaotic economic, social and political situation of apartheid in South Africa exemplified Berle's first law of power. Ultimately, Mandela's political power, built up over many years of imprisonment and interaction with others, both blacks and whites, produced a power that replaced this chaos, at least theoretically, with the power of direction. It is common knowledge that South Africa, even under the direction of Mandela and his successor, has not been able to resolve in practice such problems as ownership of property, unemployment and living conditions of the powerless. Nonetheless, the choice between chaos and power became very clear with the election of Mandela as the first nonwhite president of South Africa. The population preferred an inexperienced politician in the person of Mandela, who demanded human rights for all citizens over a candidate who, in most respects still held to the traditional view of white supremacy. This traditional approach had not achieved stability, and so the population was willing to risk an alternative. Mandela indeed fulfilled the first law of power. He filled a vacuum in the organization, thus illustrating that between chaos and power, power prevails.

Power as Personal

Power is invariably personal.   Feuerstein without doubt reflects Berle's second law of power. He decided himself, without outside assistance or persuasion, to provide financial and health benefits to his employees. No board of directors could impede or disencourage his decision. All the other Profiled Leaders, from Anthony to Mandela, also fulfilled the second law of power; namely, that it is embodied in the action of a person rather than of a group. Each acted as empowered individuals in specific contexts. Similarly, these Profiled Leaders also reflected Epstein's (1973) fourth level of power, that is, that power resides in the individual, not in the corporate entity as such.

Philosophical Direction of Power

Power is invariably based on a system of ideas or philosophy. Berle's third law is relatively easy to illustrate. All the Profiled Leaders had some ideal, concept, or philosophy upon which their exercise of power was based. One basic philosophy underpinning their actions was the power of nonviolent behavior. Another guiding principle was the need for change; however, forceful revolution as such did not enter into their thinking or their procedures to bring about that change. To begin with, the leaders Gandhi and Mandela had neither numbers of followers nor military tactical training to challenge their respective governments. This became evident when the British Establishment killed protestors in non-cooperation movements led by Gandhi. The ideology of democracy, in its various forms, permeated the thinking and actions of all the Profiled Leaders. As a human being, every person had "inalienable rights" from this perspective. (*U.S. Declaration of Independence*, 1776) In addition to these general philosophical tenets, each of these Profiled Leaders had a more specific idea of what was necessary to achieve their individual goals at the time. For example, Susan B. Anthony embraced the philosophy of the equality of women. Feuerstein replaced the classical economic model with one that recognized the proposition that human rights, in theory—and in his case, in practice—were a higher ideal and a moral imperative than were the exercise of property rights.

Role of Institutions

Power is exercised through, and depends on, institutions. The fourth of Berle's laws of power emphasizes the role of institutions in exercising power. The most obvious use of institutions to exercise power was in the case of John XXIII convoking the Vatican II Council. This important institutional gathering and its revolutionizing results could never have existed without the authoritative power structure of the Roman Catholic Church. The power and success of Cesar Chavez depended upon the ever-increasing power of the United Farm Workers to bring about change for migrant workers.   Martin Luther King, Jr. utilized organized groups, such as the National Association of Colored People (NAACP) and others, especially various churches, to recognize, acknowledge and respect the human and the civil rights of African-Americans. It should be made clear that organizations carry out the decisions of the principal power-holder. Organizations, as such, do not determine what is to be done. The power holder, whether the president of the United States, the CEO of a corporation, or the head of any institution determines what and how something is done, in either general or specific terms. Even the institution of United States Congress whose power structure is based upon the ideology of democracy, requires the signature of the President of the United States before a bill can become a law. The processes of overriding the veto of a President can be accomplished, but it is rare.

Power and Responsibility

Power is invariably confronted with, and acts in the presence of, a field of responsibility. Berle's fifth law of power—its fusion with responsibility—is probably the most acceptable and crucial to society, whether in the context of corporate, institutional or individual exercise of power. Feuerstein exemplifies the use of power as stated in Davis' Social Power Equation (1980) that the more a person has social power, the greater that person has a social responsibility to its community. As the prime employer in Lawrence, Massachusetts, he manifested throughout the history of his role, his social responsibility both to the employees and to the city. In a similar vein, Davis (1980) also proposes his Iron Law of Responsibility: if a person does not use power in a manner considered responsible by society, it will be rescinded. Post (2002) relates the Iron Law to his interpretation of the South African shift from apartheid to a unique type of democracy. These two principles, the Social Power Equation and the Iron Law of Responsibility, most clearly reflect Berle's (1969, p. 37) fifth law of power: "Power is invariably confronted with, and acts in the presence of, a field of responsibility." Thomas Aquinas (S.T II-II, q. 65, a.3, ad.1) acknowledged the possibility of losing power: "A man who abuses the power entrusted to him deserves to lose it...." Once their respective crises were addressed, Chavez and Mandela in their later years no longer had the power they had exercised earlier. Chavez lost power as an organizer of farm workers when the Teamsters Union offered a more lucrative contract to his constituents. Mandela became a symbolic father figure in South Africa rather than a political force to challenge. Both lost to some degree the charisma of their earlier years, when they were building up their power base. They were still respected as individuals who contributed much to social and political fabric of justice—but they lost their power!

As the development of the concept of power evolved in each of the Profiled Leaders, each individual became more astute and more efficient in ways to obtain power. As the rules of power become more applicable to their specific situation, the dynamism of power was channeled by individual human decisions. These decisions can guide institutions to perpetuate the guarantee of human rights and dignity. In essence, the role of power is to realize justice. (Pieper, 1965) This presentation illustrates how the power of the Profiled Leaders effected Transforming Justice.

JUSTICE

The many forms of injustice make the many forms of justice quite clear. Aristotle

The Profiled Leaders exemplify people who have addressed many kinds of injustice. Perhaps the most obvious is the injustice of those civil laws that do not respect human rights. Gandhi, King, Chavez and Mandela addressed and became victims of unjust laws. Less clear is the pursuit of Anthony, addressing suffrage as a surrogate for all rights of women. An amendment to the Bill of Rights was required to bring about the first step towards equality for women. Such equality began in the polling booth. Even less clear is the injustice of laws that pertain to the contribution to society. Taxes, especially an across-the-board sales tax and income taxes that favor the wealthy, are inequitable contributions to society. The distribution of common resources to the individual as in welfare coverage, allotments for public schools and assessments on property also can be inequitable. Thomas Aquinas (S.T. II-II, q.59, a.2) stated that injustice is twofold: first, that which is opposed to the common good of society, and he claims that all vices are ultimately against the common good; and secondly, that which refers to an inequality between two individuals.

Even the notion of the common good is disputed: Stone (1965, p.316) rejected Cahn's (1949) thesis that a personal "sense of injustice" rather than a conceptual or an objective view can provide "...only, at best, a limited number of individual particulars of what justice is not." Stone then questioned how injustices are determined. He concluded that even Gandhi's nonviolent approach to societal justice had to go beyond a subjective, personal "sense of injustice" to the development of a theory of justice that superseded the particulars of any individual's experience. Nonetheless, the common element in the injustices experienced by the Profiled Leaders is that civil law, which is supposed to lead to the common good of society, was, in fact, a source for protecting the power of the respective regimes to the detriment of some of the powerless in that society. Most people would agree that any commonly recognized injustice should be replaced with an ethically acceptable standard.

Perceptions of Justice

The Profiled Leaders also provide examples of what justice is, not only of what justice is not. How is justice perceived? Some writers conceptualize justice as rectitude, justification or even wisdom. The most popular views of justice are the *fairness* of Rawls (1971) and the *equality* of Aristotle, Aquinas and others. These might be labeled the more traditional views of justice. The equality view of Aristotle and Aquinas will be treated later in this section. Rawls

(1971) sees justice as *fairness*: under this conceptualization, the role of justice is to determine what is fair to a person, whether as an individual in isolation or as a member of a society.   With this view of justice, a disadvantaged person can depend upon the objective view of non-involved third parties to attain and perpetuate justice in the decision-making process.   Many ethicists and theologians follow Rawl's lead, especially those who propose a contemporary view of the social contract theory of justice.   (For details, refer to the social contract theory in the earlier section on rights.)

More contemporary views of justice project justice as a myriad of conceptualizations. It is purported to be a procedure, a form of compensation, a type of retribution, a political goal or even an ecumenical dimension of institutionalized religion. *Procedural* justice refers primarily to legal requirements for due process under the law; it is essentially a series of steps in a process whereby rights are recognized and respected.   Gandhi, Chavez and Mandela were denied procedural justice. It also refers to the due process that is required by ethical standards in non-legal circumstances, such as a plant closing in a one-industry city. (McMahon, 1999) *Compensatory* justice refers to the seeking of equality of those who have been harmed by civil government in cases that were considered proprietary at that time.   Possible applications include slavery in the United States, the interment of Japanese-Americans during World War II and the persecution of European Jews by Hitler's government.   In the United States affirmative action for minorities and women are considered to be a contemporary application of compensatory justice. Justice may also be *retributive* in so far as a perpetrator of injustice must make restitution to the victim.   In the United States this is usually accomplished through a monetary settlement, a jail sentence, or even capital punishment.   The execution of the terrorist Timothy McVeigh was retributive, although victims and their families in Oklahoma City may or may not have experienced retribution. How and why the death sentence is retributive is still under discussion, especially in cases in which the prisoner is frequently poor and a member of a minority group with possibly inadequate legal protection.   DNA tests have recently demonstrated the innocence of some prisoners who may have been poorly represented in the Court System.   Some critics claimed that the Mandela government-sponsored trial under the direction of Archbishop Desmond Tutu overseen by the apartheid government administrators was too lenient and not sufficiently retributive. *Ecumenical* justice is perhaps the one concept that has not been sufficiently developed to make a clear judgment on its correctness or contribution. Pope John XXIII in Vatican II attempted to restore unity and communion among all Christians, while Pope John Paul II in both his statements and his travels attempted to bridge the gap between Jews and Catholics. Both of these Popes acknowledged the mistakes of the past and sought means to resolve, at least partially, the errors that the Roman Catholic Church committed previously.

Types of Justice

The traditional view of justice, accepted even by some contemporary authorities on justice, is that justice seeks *equality*. As stated previously, this equality can be either arithmetical or proportional. The arithmetical conceptualization of equality is associated with exchange or commutative justice, as in the transaction of buying a shirt at a department store. The second or proportional viewpoint is tied to contributive justice, as in paying taxes, or distributive justice as in receiving welfare benefits. Equality should thus be taken in an analogical sense. (Finnis, 1980) A third form of equality is proposed by Catholic social thought as social justice; this is not found in classical economic liberalism. Social justice "...involves helping others to contribute...by establishing social conditions that allow and encourage participation." (Cima and Schubeck, 2001, p.225) From this perspective, social justice becomes a participatory principle; that is, people have a moral obligation to contribute to the common good. An easily understood definition of the common good is the contribution of all members of a society. Society is the aggregation of all people, including illegal immigrants and others out of the mainstream. In 1986, the Catholic bishops of the United States proposed this concept the *Pastoral Letter on Economic Justice* (par. 71) that identified and defined social justice as this type of participatory justice. Such participatory justice applies to individuals or groups. For example, Chavez exercised participatory justice as an individual, while the United Farm Workers contributed to participatory justice as a group.

For the sake of clarity, it is more appropriate to re-enumerate the four types of justice based on equality. First, commutative or exchange justice is a one-to-one interaction between persons, whether human or corporate. Secondly, distributive justice is a many-to-one interaction; through it the common good is distributed to an individual or a specified group according to some standard of proportional equality. Third, contributive justice is a one-to-many paradigm that requires an individual or specific group to contribute directly to the common good according to some standard of proportional equality. Fourth, social justice is a process in which an individual or a group participates to develop a common good in which another person or other groups can share.

Of the four kinds of justice, social justice is the most difficult to comprehend on the practical level. The parameters of social justice are wide, all embracing and not clearly bonded. As stated previously, the positive demands of social justice to help others are more difficult to ascertain than negative prohibitions, such as, do not harm others associated with other formats. But who determines "help" and "harm?" And how are they delimited? What criteria are used? To whom are they applied and from whom are they required? These and other questions confound a clear understanding of social justice. The simple but highly questionable resolution, which may be even erroneous given the lack of clear distinction, is to state that social justice is actually a form of distributive justice that applies the power of the state to bring about positive change in society. This is not the social justice that these Profiled Leaders pursued.

Finnis (1980) objects to the limiting of distributive justice to the power of the state, as many of the commentators of Aquinas do. For example, Pieper (1965, p.96) defines the common good as "...the 'social product,' the total product of community life." Indeed, "distributive justice does not authorize individuals to determine and assert on their own initiative what is due to them on the part of the social whole." To the contrary, Finnis (1980) claims that any individual in charge of an item that pertains to the common good will have duties of distributive justice. Hence any property holder can have such duties, since the goods of this earth are to be used for the good of all, not just for the individual who owns them. He also asserts that this is the true interpretation of Aquinas (S.T. II-II, q.62, a.3). Early commentators on Aquinas, like Cajetan (d. 1534) and DeSoto (d. 1560) limited distributive justice to the power of the state; that is, individuals or corporations, such as property holders, have an obligation to share what is common to every person, but this sharing is determined only through the power of the state. Pieper (1965, p.83) provides an insight when the same citation from Aquinas is translated as "...a ruler or *steward* gives to each what his rank deserves." (Italics added.) A steward has authority. Authority is one kind of power. A steward has a responsibility to deal justly with those over whom she or he has power or authority.

Executives in businesses, especially chief executive officers and presidents of corporations, are considered as stewards by many business ethicists and other business contributors. But a steward has to be granted authority and power. The question is: who appointed business executives to be stewards? Friedman (1962, p.133) raised a similar question with respect to corporate social responsibility: "Can self-selected individuals [business persons] determine what the social interest is?" The answer is not clear. But one thing is clear: women and men in business and the professions, as members of society, have a moral obligation to contribute to the common good. Some contribute through production, some through finance, some through marketing, some through research and development, and some through philanthropy. The latter may also be a form of manipulation, as it was reported by the news media at the turn of the twenty-first century, that the Miller Brewing Company, a subsidiary of R. J. Reynolds Tobacco Corporation, spent more money on advertising their philanthropy than in actual contributions to the needy. Intentionally or not, all these efforts of business contribute proportionally to the common good. However, the contribution of business has been altered since the tragic violence of September 11, 2001. As stewards, their role has become more crucial. For example, many companies had to face the dilemma of supporting employees versus cutting staff to protect their companies from bankruptcy. The loss of jobs has become a serious contemporary problem in the United States. Fortunately, this issue was not discernible in the cases of the Profiled Leaders but offers an opportunity for new leaders to apply the concept of Transforming Justice.

Naturalist Fallacy

Finnis (1980) may be equating reality—what a corporate executive or property owner "is"—to the normative what a person "ought" to do as a just person. If this is correct (and anyone who interprets another can easily be challenged), this might be considered a "naturalist fallacy" of going from " what is" (a corporate executive or property owner) to what "ought to be" (a person with economic power who uses power to bring about "economic justice"). According to Finnis (1980, p.33), a person with personal power, such as property owners, "...will have duties of distributive justice; hence any property-holder can have such duties [as sharing]." But what is the source of this obligation?   This question was not a problem for Feuerstein: without any philosophical elaboration, but certainly with religious conviction, he exercised the highest form of distributive justice. He contributed generously to those in need, one of the most acceptable criteria for distributive justice. He provided security and loyalty to his employees and to the city of Lawrence, Massachusetts. Although the theory of distributive justice is not clearly applied to individuals (traditionally, only the state—not society or individuals—determines how the common good should be shared and with whom), the decision of Feuerstein illustrates a superb practical application. He simply acted on his convictions as a humane and socially conscious employer. This case illustrates that Transforming Justice is operative. It does not deal with the theoretical *per se,* but with the practical, as all the Profiled Leaders clearly illustrated in their actions, be these marches, boycotts, demonstrations or fasts. They manifested the "here and now" approach to Transforming Justice. They all held that humans, whoever and wherever, have basic rights that no one, not governments nor those holding opposing ideologies, can ignore or not respect.

Commutative Justice

The concept of commutative or exchange justice is the most acceptable to classical economists and contemporary communitarians, that is, those who see justice, even commutative justice, as having a social dimension. Most people experience commutative or exchange justice in their daily activities, such as when buying groceries, purchasing gasoline for the automobile or receiving wages from an employer for services rendered. Commutative justice is a one-to-one exchange. It is frequently the exchange of money for a product or service. There are two considerations about commutative justice that should be reviewed. First, commutative justice does contribute to the common good of society, but only indirectly.   As relational, justice is social by its very nature. Its primary object is to equalize the rights and obligations of the parties in a bilateral contract. It can hardly be doubted that Feuerstein's explicit unilateral (instead of the traditional bilateral) contract with his employees after the factory fire did have a positive societal effect on the city of Lawrence, Massachusetts.   His Transforming Justice went far beyond the traditional classic liberalism of many business executives and managers.   Cima and Schubeck (2001, p.224), state that classical economic liberalism claims: "[I]f an imperative cannot be codified and established as law, it is not justice." As will be illustrated later, this position is an application of the Positive Law theory. Basically, it means: if there is no law, there is no justice.

In commutative justice, a person primarily obtains equality through power, as seen in the employer-employee relationship. Both members of this dyad possess at least some economic power. The employer has economic power as a property owner or as an executive who controls the corporation. The employee has economic power in as much as she or he contributes a "value added" component to the enterprise. The same can be seen in distributive justice, insofar as a person (for example, the mayor of a large city) or a group (such as the organized American Association of Retired Persons) require political power to establish equality among the constituents or members, and, therefore, to attain justice. A person can only exemplify and exercise contributive justice when that person has the capacity, that is, the power—economic, political, social or moral power—to bring about equality. Power is also required in social justice situations. Its application depends upon the particular circumstances of time and place. The Profiled Leaders applied their power in particular times, places and contexts. Their precise use of power established a causal relationship towards the attainment of each one's particular form of Transforming Justice. All of the Profiled Leaders exemplified some form of power in their commitment to justice. In each situation, a consistent just result occurred.

Theories of Justice

Bird (1967) presents a dialectical view of the concept of justice. He claims that throughout history, all theories of justice have three aspects in common: first, justice is a social norm; second, justice is approbative; third, justice is obligatory. As stated previously, justice is relational and by that fact it is social. Justice is obligatory, either by law or by ethical standards. By approbative, Bird explains (p.13): "Since the evaluation in terms of justice is always positive in that it shows approval, it can be said that justice is an approbative concept." By approbative, he means that all three theories of justice presented in his book, *The Idea of Justice,* perceive justice as positive. Justice is an accepted and approved form of good; it is not associated with a form of evil. Finally, all theories state that some form of obligation ensues from positive law, from social standards or from the very nature of the situation.

Bird classifies all theories of justice into three categories. First, Positive Law theory states that justice and injustice are dependent exclusively upon positive law. Law itself is independent of justice; indeed, positive law determines what justice is: no law, no justice as such. Bird claims that Austin, Clark, Hobbes, Holmes, and Spinoza, among others, subscribe to this theory. Second, the Social Good theory states that justice and injustice are not exclusively dependent on positive law, but are derived exclusively from society.

As such, these do not just spring from natural rights, but exist ultimately to promote the common good. Thus society takes precedence over the individual, and consequently determines a person's basic rights. He places Bentham, Blandshard, Hume, Mill, Pound, Sidgwick and others in this category. However, he is cautious not to label this classical Utilitarian theory, specifically purporting the greatest good for the greatest number. Bird also includes Rawls in the Social Good theory, as Rawls perceives justice as stemming from a social contract. However, it should be noted that Bird's presentation was based on articles that Rawls wrote before he published his widely acclaimed book, *A Theory of Justice* (1971). Third, Bird states that in the Natural Right theory, justice provides a criterion of positive law. This position is based on the concept that natural human rights come before positive law. As such, they determine whether positive law is just. The long list of contributors to this literature associated with this ideology are: Aquinas, Aristotle, Augustine, Blackstone, Brunner, Cicero, Frankena, Grotius, Jefferson, Kant, Leibniz, Locke, Maritain, Messner, Plato, Pufendorf, Ryan, Scheler, Suarez, DelVecchio, Vitoria, Wilson and Wolf. Other more contemporary theorists who can be added to this list of classical authors, are ethicists and moral theologians, such as Finnis (1980) and McBrien (1980). These contemporary authors perceive natural law from a more open-ended perspective derived from historical development. The traditional natural law supporters build upon a more classical concept, namely, that nature in itself is sufficient and as such does not need any further development. They do not acknowledge the different applications that have occurred within historical context. For example, the perception of two hundred years ago that slaves were property or chattel has developed over time to the current view that slavery is an infringement of human rights and therefore unjust.

Theories and Transforming Justice

The question at this point is: *how do these theories of justice relate to Transforming Justice?* To answer this, it is necessary to reiterate Bird's concepts of justice. Transforming Justice incorporates in its concept the three notions of justice as a social norm, approbative and obligatory.

a. *Transforming Justice and Positive Law Theory*

As a concept, Transforming Justice rejects the Positive Law theory. Anthony, Gandhi, King and Chavez challenged existing positive laws through civil disobedience. They did not accept civil laws that did not recognize the existence of specific human rights in certain people. They abhorred ethnic, sexual, racial or social class profiling. In each of these cases there were existing laws that forbade the exercise of specific human rights. Those in power refused to acknowledge the human rights of these profiled people; they determined that only positive law provided justice by enumerating what rights the law would grant and what the law would deny. Stone (1965, p.123) states that Blackstone was "... the arch-sanctifier of the legal *status quo*." Blackstone believed that English law could not be improved. He even believed that it incorporated natural law! In order to change this approach to justice, old laws had to be revised or new laws created, as illustrated in the replacement of the apartheid law in South Africa with a more democratic approach. The Profiled Leaders, through their persistent efforts, did bring about a change in the civil laws of India, South Africa and the United States. In all of these cases, justice became a criterion for positive, civil law. Thus, existing civil law was not the only standard for justice. Each exercised Transforming Justice by challenging the particular civil law that restrained human rights in a specific situation. Any of those profiled could not have challenged the existing civil law under the Positive Law theory. They could, as could anyone, disobey it. But there was no apparent means to challenge an existing law except through fasting, boycotts, marches, non-cooperation and other acts that led to civil disobedience.

Thus, Transforming Justice clearly rejects the Positive Law theory that justice is dependent only upon civil law for its existence. For the positivists, law comes before justice and is the only source of justice. For them, without law justice is merely subjective. It is civil law that is deemed objective. As subjective, justice as such cannot "judge" positive law. Positive Law theory also rejects the traditional definition of justice, " to render to each person what is due," unless "what is due" is granted by civil law. Thus, Positive Law proponents claim that this position of determining "what is due to the other" leads to a very subjective view of justice.

This theory, however, appears to ignore that civil laws can be interpreted differently, as Judge Frank Johnson did in the cases of the boycotts and marches of Dr. Martin Luther King, Jr. He appealed to the higher law of the U.S. Constitution and, in so doing, he overruled Alabama state law. The Positive Law theory thus denies the existence of natural rights. Rather, it purports that all rights come from civil law, the only objective norm. An aspect of Positive Law theory "...rests on might (to have conformity to the law), it is also based on the approval and agreement of the men (*sic*) who live under it." (Bird, 1967, p.69) In fact, this theory might go so far as to propose that justice depends upon power, as Thrasymachus wrote. (Woodhead, 1970) This theory also states that when justice is not equated with legality, it becomes not only subjective but also indeterminate. This is a common criticism of the Positive Law theorists towards the Social Good and the Natural Right theories of justice. According to the Positive Law theory of justice, the "just" person is one who obeys civil law—period. As stated previously, the Positive Law theory *as such*, contributes little, if anything, to Transforming Justice. With respect to the Profiled Leaders, positive law was oppressive; it did not recognize the human rights of its legitimate citizens.

The proponents of Transforming Justice, such as those detailed in the Profiles, do not, and cannot by definition, support the Positive Law theory. Why? First of all, the Profiled Leaders challenged the position that civil law as such is neither just nor unjust. The fallacy is that if justice depends only upon the law, then there are no unjust laws, since justice and injustice come from positive law. In this conceptualization law comes before justice. In the cases of the Profiled Leaders, all except Johnson and Feuerstein were convinced that it was reasonable to act contrary to the positive law in their respective situations. Johnson was of the opinion that laws denying human rights were unjust and should be challenged. This view directly opposed the position of Positive Law theory, which required obedience to the law even in Alabama where segregation was legally enforced. Feuerstein went beyond the mandates of positive law, which he could easily have invoked, received insurance, and liquidated his business, as appropriate in his situation. By recognizing the basic human rights of his employees to work and by broadening their application to include a yearly bonus, Feuerstein exercised his rights as an owner to a determinate and objective form of justice that went beyond positive law. The actions of the other Profiled Leaders were also determinate related to what they were trying to achieve. The question is: were they subjective and perhaps emotional, rather than objective and determinate, as is required in the Positive Law theory? The proponents of the Positive Law theory would insist that questions about justice in the profiles were subjective. They do accept the proposition that law, and ultimately justice, depends upon society and varies according to the constituents of that society. Law often follows social movements. For example, civil rights causes preceded civil rights legislation. The Profiled Leaders clearly illustrate the various constituents of society in varied environments: India, South Africa, the Vatican, and the United States. One thing is certain: all those profiled would clearly reject the basic tenet of the Positive Law theory that law is the only source of justice. Even Johnson, who presented an unprecedented interpretation of Constitutional Law as applied to the states, and Feuerstein, who acted contrary to classical economic liberalism, challenged the system and implicitly, if not explicitly, rejected the Positive Law theory of justice.

b. *Social Good Theory*

The Social Good theory of justice holds that society, not the law, is the source of justice. This theory excludes both positive (civil) and natural (inborn) law as the only source of justice. It is society that determines who has rights and who does not have rights. This is based upon some form of agreement among the participants. It is a *conventional* relation. As such, there exist no innate natural rights. Indeed, any unjust law stems "...from the fact that it goes counter to the social good of the group whose law it is." (Bird, 1967, p.80) Society at first denied the civil rights of Anthony, King and Chavez in the United States. Society also denied civil rights to Gandhi in India and Mandela in South Africa. Society in these cases was the government—the state---that reflected the attitudes of most of their respective constituents (or those in power) by enacting laws that directly denied or limited certain civil rights and indirectly restricted human rights. But society changes. What society grants, society can take away. The basic human right to meet with other citizens was rescinded during Mandela's detention as a prisoner on Robbin Island in South Africa. Society may also grant civil rights, the goal of Anthony's persistent effort to obtain voting rights for women. Gradually, when under pressure to reexamine its laws, society granted civil rights to the Indians, the South Africans, and the Americans of every race, gender and economic level.

For some proponents of the Social Good theory, justice may contain natural or innate elements, but what is essential is the subordination of justice to society in such a way that all its principles are ultimately dependent upon society and its needs. (Bird, 1967) Furthermore, equality might be important in the analysis of justice, but it is not basic. "If equality supplies a criterion of justice, it does so because it is itself conducive to the common good of society." (Bird, 1967, p.99) From this perspective, the search for and attainment of proportional equality by the Profiled Leaders did indeed lead ultimately to the common good of society.

The position of the Social Good proponents views equality from a significantly different perspective than that of Aquinas (S.T., II-II, q. 57, a.1.) who states: "[I]t is proper to justice...to direct man in his relations with others: because it denotes a kind of equality, as its very nature implies; indeed we are wont to say that things are adjusted when they are made equal, for equality is in reference of one thing to some others." For Aquinas, equality is intrinsic to the concept of justice; it does not accrue from an agreement among social forces. Thomas Aquinas, consistent with Aristotle, insisted that equals should be treated equally. Being treated equally in contracts between individuals as in commutative or exchange justice, which is arithmetical, differs significantly from equality in contributive and distributive justice, which is proportional to the needs or capacity of the person.

A problem with the Social Good theory arises when determining the parameters of the "common good" and of the "society." These are not clearly defined in our expanding global economy. What might be judged by society to be equitable and just in an industrialized country might not be such in a developing country. Viewing the media coverage of the September 11, 2001 attacks on the New York City World Trade Towers and the Pentagon in Washington, D.C., simultaneous with the demonstrations of approval in Pakistan illustrate how differently equality is perceived by different societies. The Muslim extremists subscribe to the notion that inequality exists and should be eradicated by efficient, albeit violent, means, regardless of whether such means are unethical or promote religious fanaticism. It should be recalled that Mandela permitted, and even encouraged, guerilla warfare, but he denounced and forbade terrorist acts leveled against innocent civilians in his steps toward equality in South Africa. Notably, the goal of equality and democracy in India and in South Africa was different from the practice of equality and democracy in the United

States. It appears that at least in theory, the developing countries ascribe to a more distributive view of equality than the prevailing view in the United States.

At this juncture it might be useful to consider two concepts from the realm of marketing in an attempt to delineate the parameters between the common good and society. Two notions from marketing are *product* and *market share*. The first question marketers ask is what is a clear definition of the product. DuPont faced this problem when the company was accused of monopolizing the product of cellophane; it had well over 80% share of this market. DuPont argued that the product was not cellophane itself, but really flexible packaging material, like plastic and butchers' paper. When cellophane is considered to be a type of flexible packaging material, DuPont controlled less than 20% of this market. Thus, DuPont did not have a monopoly according to civil law in the United States. By taking this category perspective in its defense, DuPont received a favorable decision from the United States Supreme Court in its antitrust case. In a similar analysis, we can ask what is the "product" of the common good? Related to Transforming Justice, the specific "product" or desired output was conceived differently by each of the Profiled Leaders. In a more generalized sense, at the level of a category, however, the common "product" was "equality." This could either be defined as arithmetic (as in the case of Feuerstein) or as proportional (when related to Gandhi, King, Chavez, and Mandela). All those profiled sought some form of equality.

The second marketing variable relates to market share. Market share can be dramatically different in one region (city, county, state, national, international) than in another. What might be a monopoly in a relatively small city like Kenosha, Wisconsin, might be an oligopoly or a minority interest in a larger metropolis like Chicago, Illinois. For example, beer sales in Busch Stadium in St. Louis are limited to Busch products; there is no competition from other brands of beer. However, Busch products do have to compete with similar products in the larger market outside the stadium in retail stores, bars and restaurants. Each of the Profiled Leaders focused upon attaining success in the form of a large market share of a smaller market segment. Anthony focused upon the segment of women, Pope John XXIII related primarily to Roman Catholics and secondarily to all Christians and to other religious groups, while Chavez focused upon farm workers, and Feuerstein with employees at Malden Mills. Consequently, the Transforming Justice of each did not address the same broad market as the other Profiled Leaders. For example, Gandhi and King had widespread influence throughout the entire world; they became the prototypes for nonviolent change.

From the above presentation, it is still uncertain who determines what the common good is, who ascertains what is meant by society, and who has the power to effect justice. The Social Good theory thus has limited value in its application to Transforming Justice.

c. *Natural Right Theory*

The third approach to justice is what Bird (1967) calls the Natural Right theory. He eschews the use of the Natural Law theory because, for in his presentation, *law* is applied exclusively to positive law. Instead of natural *law*, he prefers the concept of natural *right*. In terms of the perception of justice, rights are the material of justice. The purpose of justice is to recognize and acknowledge rights so that they may be brought to fruition and exercised. Most proponents of the Natural Right theory, however, subscribe to the Natural Law theory as well. The Latin word *jus* is translated most commonly to mean "right," or "law." The two translations are frequently considered to be interchangeable. Aquinas (S.T., q.58, a.1.) accepted, with minor adjustment (*i.e.,* justice as a *moral* virtue), the famous definition of justice is that proposed by the Roman jurist Ulpian (*Dig.,* I, 1,10, pr.): *justice is a habit whereby a man (sic) renders to each one his due by a constant and perpetual will.* Furthermore, Aquinas states that his definition is "...about the same definition as that given by the Philosopher (Aristotle)." Aquinas also states that Ulpian's definition postulates an act "...instead of the habit, which takes its species from that act, because habit implies relation to act." (S.T. II-II, q. 58, a.1.) In more popular terms, justice is operative. DelVecchio (1956, p.73) provided another insight into this definition when he wrote: "For the Roman jurist...law and right can and must always be sought for less in the detailed rules of the laws than in their foundation, that is, in the intrinsic nature of things, which is a perennial and inexhaustible source." Indeed, McBrien (1980, p.994) wrote that: "For the Greeks, this [natural] law is entirely apart from us. Reality is a given. We must simply conform ourselves to it. The Romans, on the other hand, were activists...shakers and movers, so to speak...tended to be innovative." The Greeks reflected the classicist mentality of conforming to the "given" of nature. The Romans reflect a more historically conscious mentality. According to the Greeks, man must obey the classicist natural law, since it transcends him in every respect. (Stone, 1967) On the contrary, the Romans conceived natural law chiefly to the juridical and legal orders so that "...[T]he natural right, or the just by nature, ...became the *ius natural* of the Roman jurists, i.e., a speculative body of universal moral ideas and principles." (Brown, 1967, p.252) Stone (1967, p.43) made an interesting observation when he wrote: "The universalism in these Greco-Roman concepts [of natural law] was horizontal across peoples and did not penetrate vertically down to the subject classes, for instance, of slaves." Christianity as such did not oppose this horizontal application of the natural law, but it always has had a concern for the poor, the weak and the powerless.

Going from the Natural Right theory to the Natural Law theory is more than a giant step forward. Some might say that it is actually a step backward. It can be compared to crossing a chasm. A more fitting analogy might be that of a small motorboat buffeted in a sea of challenging waves of utilitarianism, pragmatism, liberalism, positivism, individualism, communitarianism, Marxism and other "-isms" of this ilk proposed during the Enlightenment and the

Industrial Revolution. These and other theories, such as evolution and its later question of physics, attempted to replace natural law with empirically grounded conceptions of what a human being is and what is his or her role in society.

Bird (1967, p.120) states: "...the Natural Right position does not always in fact involve an assertion of natural law." There is no doubt that some proponents of the Positive Law and Social Good theories, which do not subscribe to natural rights, would support the Natural Law theory. For example, Stone (1967) mentions that there are certain quasi-absolutes of justice but denies that they belong to, or derive from, any natural law. He is skeptical of postulating a natural law from what might be a natural right. Bird (1967) accepts Stone as a Natural Right practitioner, but denies that he subscribes to the natural law. Finnis (1980) rejects Stone as a proponent for any natural right or law. For others, the problem lies in the terminology: a right is a fact, while a law is a norm. How does a person go from a fact to a norm?

This abrupt shift from a fact to a norm is called the naturalist fallacy. (It was treated briefly in the exposition on distributive justice.) "It is best described as the fallacy of deriving an *ought* statement from premises consisting entirely of *is* statements." (Bird, 1967, p.32) Critics of the Natural Law theory claim that just because a person is or possesses a role or attribute does not guarantee that the person ought to act in a specific way. They also state that to have an ought in a conclusion requires at least one ought in the premises; that is, no number of *is* statements by themselves can validly yield an *ought* statement and, consequently, no ethical conclusion can be derived from non-ethical premises. For example, Americans have a constitutional right to life. This is the "is" statement. But it cannot be inferred that everyone ought to have access to every form of life-giving medical care at any cost. This is the "ought" statement. Proponents of the Natural Law theory respond by quoting Aquinas' first principle of the practical order: good is to be done; evil is to be avoided. This norm comes from the practical order; it is not a theoretical conclusion. Finnis (1980, p.33) states that these first "ought" principles are self-evident and indemonstrable. He embellishes this position with strong statements about these "ought" principles: "They are not inferred from speculative principles. They are not inferred from facts. They are not inferred from metaphysical propositions about human nature, or about the nature of good and evil, or about 'the function of a human being, nor are they inferred from the teleological [i.e., emphasizing the end or goal] conception of nature or any other conceptions of nature." These first principles can be adequately grasped by anyone with the age and use of reason. Indeed, they are self-evident and, in this sense, are intuited. (Bird, 1967)

How does this exposition of the naturalist fallacy relate to the Profiled Leaders? There does not seem to be any direct relevance. Nonetheless, each of those profiled illustrated the belief that every human being has rights and dignity. Recall how Gandhi always made a distinction between the inhumane rule of the British Establishment and the rights and dignity of its administrators as human beings. Similarly in the United States, Anthony, King and Chavez sought to implement their inalienable rights as humans within an unsympathetic and sometimes barbarous (as in the King challenge) societal context. For these Profiled Leaders, their basic orientation toward humanity did not come as a conclusion from a theoretical premise. It came from the practical order that required good be done and evil be avoided.

Natural law may be understood as the obligation perceived by those of reason to conform to nature (the classic mentality), or the obligation, built into nature, to use moral judgment (historical consciousness). Contemporary ethicists and moral theologians consider natural law to be open-ended to historical development. Even some of the more traditional academics, like MacIntyre (1988, p.195), admit that the universal principles "...do require in numerous particular types of occasion supplementation in order to have right application." (S.T., I-II, 94, 5) McBrien (1980, p. 943) goes a step further when he wrote that "[C]lassicism neglects the basic Thomistic [Aquinas] principle 'whatever is received is received according to the mode [situation] of the receiver." (S.T. I-II, q.79, a.6) He called this historically conditioned concept of justice "Transcendental Thomism." It is open to history and, perhaps, other social sciences. The problem with this approach is the possibility of subjective relativism, the belief that the only basic norms are those individually acknowledged. Another problematic issue is the perspective that all laws, including natural law, are irrelevant. McBrien (1980, p.941) states that "[T]he values (e.g., the dignity of the human life) may be absolute, but the norms to realize them (e.g., no killing) are relative to the historical situation." Thus, they are more inductive than deductive, as the profiles exemplify. The historical recognition of human dignity by Anthony is different from the perception of human dignity by Mandela and the others. Each perceived it within the historical context of his or her time. Each came from the basic inclinations (Maritain, 1949) that are experienced in concrete situations and which are manifested only through history and thus are susceptible to development and progress. Fuchs (1965, p.57) wrote: "...natural law statements are not exhaustive judgments on man as he actually exists. They are all the same true and valid...[natural law] demands a consideration of the historical peculiarities of society, that is, of certain people and groups in human community." Stone (1965) suggested that it is the "prudence" proposed by Aquinas that produces a "flexibility" which is expected in concrete situations, especially those experienced in various historical milieus. McBrien (1980, p.979) states: "Prudence does not answer the question: 'What is the best way in principle to do the right thing?' Rather: 'What is the best way for me, in this situation, to do the right thing?'" Perhaps the most authoritative statement about the openness of natural law came indirectly from a statement in the Vatican II document on the "Church in the Modern World": "Thus, the human race has passed from a rather static concept of reality to a more dynamic, evolutionary one." The commentator of the Abbott translation suggested in footnote 11 (p. 204) that

"[T]he reference to dynamic forces here is perhaps one reason why some critics early objected to the influence of Pierre Teilhard deChardin on the document." DeChardin was a progressive philosopher, anthropologist, sociologist and theologian. McBrien (1980, p.1073) wrote: "No Christian spiritual writer contributed more substantially to that new emphasis than Teilhard deChardin (d. 1955)." The Catholic theologians Rahner and Lonergan also provided strong support to this historical perspective of natural law. MacIntyre (1988, p.194) presents a slightly different approach: "So the practice of the virtue of justice yields a knowledge of this kind [experiential rather than cognitive], including a knowledge of the precepts of the natural law." Thus, historical consciousness does not transform the basic tenets of the Natural Law theory. It does not take on the role of adaptation or change in the Natural Law theory. It is rather an application or adjustment that is experienced with changing conditions.

The flexibility in the historical consciousness approach to natural law can be traced to Aquinas in his exposition on prudence. He presents the construct of a flexible prudence both in the framing of general principles of natural law and in the application of these conditions to changing situations. Indeed, Pieper (1965, p.34) states: "Prudent decision is the 'measure' of a concrete moral act."

Critics reject natural law for three reasons: variability, indefiniteness, and mode of justification. Its variability shows that there is no general, changing agreement about the content of natural law. This is exemplified in the dramatic change in attitude and law towards chattel slavery of African-Americans in the United States. Bird (1967, p.176) counteracts stating: "Opinions can vary without the object of the opinion itself varying." All of the Profiled Leaders subscribed to the principle that respect was due to all human beings; they differed, at times dramatically, in actualizing this respect. The feminist view of Anthony differed substantially from the distributive justice view of Feuerstein.

The second criticism, indefiniteness, rests on the position that natural rights are too vague to provide a norm for human conduct. However, through historical development, people can more clearly perceive what is a natural right, as, for example, in the injustice of chattel slavery and the justice of women's equality with men. The marches and boycotts of Gandhi, King and Chavez, the imprisonment of Mandela and the convocation of Vatican II by John XXIII were all events that can never be accused of being vague.

Critics finally claim that natural right and natural law cannot be justified because it has no objective basis upon which a disinterested person could verify or confirm the findings. In response to this criticism, natural law subscribers conclude that there is a norm for what is due to a person as a person. An individual need only realize what it means to be human and then postulate the right to life. In other words, this human life has to be respected in a manner different from other living things and that this life cannot be unjustly taken without serious reasons justification, if at all.

According to Aquinas (S.T., I-II, q.95, a.2), positive laws are related to natural law either as a conclusion from the principles or a determination of something more common.   For example, both the prohibition against murder and its punishment belong to the natural law.   The prohibition of murder is a conclusion from the principle that evil must not be done.   The punishment for committing murder is a particular determination made by positive law. Compensation is also a determination of civil law.   Wu (1967, X, p.257) took this idea a step further when he wrote that there is no clear-cut borderline between natural law and human law: "That is why St. Thomas [Aquinas] maintains that the natural law can be changed by way of addition and is capable of unlimited growth."   This notion fits well into the historical consciousness approach to natural law, presented previously.   He also stated: "... it is a conclusion of the natural law that he who injures another should compensate him; but exactly how to compensate him is a determination that can be laid down by positive law and is subject to change." (1967, X, p.257) However, the lives of the Profiled Leaders illustrate that positive law, which these prominent individuals challenged, was ultimately considered by society to be against human nature and thus against the natural law.   Civil law in the United States, India and South Africa had to be changed to meet this basic need.   Nonetheless, retributive justice or punishment is not the same as compensatory justice, that is, how to make up a loss.   The awards granted to the Japanese-Americans who were interred in World War II was compensatory, but the fact of the internment was a punishment for being of Japanese descent.   The threat of a similar injustice has been a concern of the American Muslims after the terrorist attacks on the United States.   Pieper (1965) viewed the *restitutio* of Aquinas as *re*-storation, *re*-compense, or *re*-tuning.   The purpose of restitution is to restore balance, that is, to restore some form of equality.   It seems that the action of some of the Profiled Leaders was *re*-tuning society to recognize human rights.   They did not attempt to *re*-store what they did not have; they never had recognition of their human rights in the first place.   Nor did they, at that time, demand or expect some form of *re*-compense.   For the most part, they simply wanted recognition of their rights as human beings and as citizens of a just state.   Ultimately, their efforts prevailed.

This rather long and detailed exposition on justice leads to one important conclusion: natural law is basic to an understanding of Transforming Justice.

CHAPTER 4

Formal Definition, Observations And Conclusions

Formal Definition

After many examples, a detailed discussion of the requisite elements and a review of various theories related to these elements, it is now appropriate to offer a formal definition of our focal construct. It is the following:

> *Transforming Justice is the capacity to effect change in society, through ethically derived power, in order for people to exercise their human rights or claims on others.*

Observations

The following paragraphs offer several reflective observations that connect the Profiled Leaders to the focus of this book—Transforming Justice. This Observations Section will be classified into nine relevant factors affecting each Profiled Leader's attainment of Transforming Justice. They include: 1) Focus; 2) Nonviolence; 3) Power; 4) Economic Impact; 5) Weaknesses; 6) Civil Disobedience; 7) Moral Imagination; 8) Visualization: Venn diagram; and 9) Liberation Theology. Civil Disobedience and Moral Imagination will be developed more extensively than the others. Power will be covered only as a component of Transforming Justice.

1. **Focus.** In the case of all the Profiled Leaders, a single person was instrumental in initiating the process that brought about Transforming Justice. Each person, with the exception of John XXIII and Feuerstein, focused ultimately upon injustice related to a specific group. Anthony limited her actions to women. Chavez sought to protect farm workers, particularly Hispanic migrant

workers. In contrast, Feuerstein used his economic power to respect the human rights of his employees and community; as such, he did not correct injustices. The scope of Transforming Justice in the above three cases was very limited in its application.   Johnson and King developed a Transforming Justice that primarily focused on race, specifically Afro-Americans in the United States. Although the means used to bring about Transforming Justice were employed primarily in the Southeastern United States, their effect was nationwide. Gandhi and Mandela directly focused on the populations of their respective countries and on altering the structure of their governments in broad contexts.   The nonviolence of Gandhi towards the British Establishment and the peaceful transition from apartheid to democracy in South Africa became models of significance to the whole world and thus had global impact. However, Pope John XXIII's focus was unique: he managed to enlarge the scope and perspective of the Catholic Church with respect to the larger world.   Some might argue that he attempted to correct a number of the injustices perpetrated by the Catholic Church on various groups.

Anthony, Gandhi, King and Mandela were originally more scattered in defining their goals related to a particular group of people. At first they were involved in a number of causes, but ultimately funneled their efforts toward the pursuit of a single objective. Mandela originally had a number of interrelated goals, but later he realized he could achieve more if he focused his activities. Ultimately, he based his actions toward one premise: if apartheid could be transformed to some form of democracy, the recognition of human and civil rights would follow. Anthony thought that women's right to vote would open the way for feminine equality in many walks of life. Gandhi believed that if the British Establishment were removed, India would be "free." Chavez believed that unionization would solve the problems of the migrant workers.   King assumed that a change in civil right laws would change the legal status of African-Americans. Unlike the other people profiled, John XXIII, Judge Frank Johnson and Aaron Feuerstein focused upon specific actions from the beginning of their process to obtain Transforming Justice. Clear focus was ultimately necessary. Like a view through binoculars, most of the Profiled Leaders had to "keep adjusting" until their focus became clear.

2. Nonviolence.   All the Profiled Leaders believed in and pursued nonviolent means to attain their goals. Nonviolence was undoubtedly the most pervasive means for obtaining Transforming Justice.   Even before Gandhi, who is considered the father of the nonviolence movement, Susan B. Anthony espoused this strategy, possibly due to her Quaker upbringing. She nonetheless allowed a form of violence, one time only, in her quest for constitutional equality for women. Although violence did also occur in some of the marches and boycotts under Gandhi, King and Chavez, it was incidental; it might have been foreseen as a possibility, maybe even a likelihood, as in the King marches, but it was not planned or desired. As stated previously, Mandela at first attempted to transform the South African government with nonviolent means. Ultimately he permitted the violence of guerilla warfare, but he rejected terrorism as a means to obtain his goals. In the final analysis, it was nonviolence in the form of economic boycotts by foreign business investment that sealed the fate of apartheid. Accompanying nonviolence, prayer, meditation, contemplation and fasting were incorporated by some of these Profiled Leaders as a silent form of nonviolence. These practices created an unsuspecting power for transformation. Sometimes they even became the occasion for civil disobedience.

3. **Power.** In each of these cases the overriding concern was to "transform," that is, to bring about notable change in a particular situation in society. To bring about such change, each person used some form of power. As stated previously, the power in each case was obtained differently. In the case of Malden Mills, Feuerstein had economic power related to his inherited role. He directed it towards safeguarding his employees' security in salaries, health insurance and employment. Pope John XXIII automatically received ecclesiastical power upon his election as pope. Gandhi, King, Mandela, Chavez, and Anthony gradually accumulated sufficient power to "transform" human rights into justice. This building up of power required time and persistence, as all except Feuerstein, John XXIII and Judge Johnson experienced.

Obtaining sufficient power to transform some aspect of society was a process. However, the process to obtain power required different means in various times and contexts. Mandela's shift from nonviolence to guerilla warfare was the most radical means for obtaining power. It was effective, but it could be questioned whether the identical goal of freedom might have been obtained through nonviolence. This, of course, cannot be answered with any certitude. However, it did demonstrate that obtaining power can be done in a number of ways.

Theory (such as non-violence) had to undergo changes as circumstances changed. In another example, Dr. Martin Luther King, Jr.'s strong social power at Selma differed significantly from the exercise of his limited power in the Rosa Parks boycott. In the Rosa Parks boycott he assumed a minor role, but later at Selma he had increased his presence and power nationally, making him more instrumental in bringing about change. King applied the "freedoms" of the First Amendment of the Bill of Rights, as interpreted by Judge Johnson. On the contrary, Feuerstein's economic power and John XXIII's papal power were obtained automatically related to their roles, Feuerstein through family ownership and Pope John through Church dogma and canon law.

4. **Economic Impact.** The Malden Mills and Mandela cases had a direct economic impact in the process of bringing about Transforming Justice. Feuerstein's action had direct economic consequences on his employees and the

larger local community. The rejection of apartheid by the industrial nations affected production, trade, financial security and stability in South Africa. The other cases had more indirect economic consequences. The impact of the other Profiled Leaders seems to have a more indirect effect on their communities. For example, the Chavez-led boycotts of grapes and lettuce seriously affected the economies of local property owners. It also had, at that time, a direct negative effect on some wholesale and retail sales in the produce and fruit industries. Indirectly, it affected the economy of national and even international societies through a form of the "domino theory." Thus, both direct and indirect economic impacts contributed to change in the structure of their communities.

5. **Weaknesses.** Except Johnson, all the Profiled Leaders through personal indiscretions, lack of communication or some other weakness created "road blocks" to obtaining their goals. These faults were sometimes personal, such as whether Pope John's "inspiration" to convoke Vatican Council II came directly to him from God at that time or had simply developed as appropriate for the time. (Hebblethwaite, 1985) Nonetheless, the Profiled Leader's weaknesses did not directly affect his or her commitment to the pursuit of rights and justice. Each had a drive towards articulated goals that not even imprisonment could diminish. As mentioned previously, Anthony allowed some violence, as did Mandela. Gandhi was accused of favoring the powerful. King allegedly had sexual indiscretions. Chavez isolated himself from the workers and employed inefficient family members as administers of the union. Feuerstein did not patent his Polartec fabric. It can be said that each of the Profiled Leaders mentioned had human foibles and imperfections, or a "toe of clay". Their effectiveness in the long run is an indication that they did not have "feet" of clay. With a single toe removed, a person generally does not lose balance! A person does not lose focus because of such a weakness; rather it can even be a strengthening force. The apostle Paul stated in the second letter to the Corinthians that he was strong because the power of God sustained him when he was weak. Perhaps it was in their weaknesses that these Profiled Leaders realized their need for power, no matter from whence it came, directly or indirectly, but always within the bounds of human dignity.

Anthony, Gandhi, Chavez and Mandela had to compete with others to attain their goals. Anthony had rivals in publishing. Gandhi challenged Nehru's violent approach. Mandela had a rival political organization that challenged his universal membership in the organization. Furthermore, his rivals wanted a black-only country while Mandela insisted on a multi-racial society. Chavez lost members of the United Farm Workers to a competing union. John XXIII had some serious opposition from the Roman Curia to his type of council. The Roman Curia is the actual ruling body governing the Roman Catholic Church. With almost unlimited power, it determines the practical applications of what the members of this Church should believe, how they are to believe it, and what is moral or immoral. All the Profiled Leaders had to face and overcome what might be considered a "weakness" in the attainment of their ultimate goals. The so-called weakness of each Profiled Leader might have been a detour, rather than a rejection, in the path towards attaining their goals.

Each of those profiled demonstrates complete commitment to such a goal, but with the existence of some human weakness. This is labeled "the fundamental option." It has been, but need not be, exclusively a theological concept. It is based upon the human freedom to make an irrevocable choice toward something or someone, and is frequently applied to commitment to God. Everything subsequent derives its meaning and "reason for being" from such a commitment. For example, marriage is a commitment that affects every act a married person performs. What before marriage might be a concern for the individual, such as health, profession or education, after the commitment of marriage becomes part of the resources for creating a new family unit. However, this commitment does not rule out the possibility, more likely the probability, of acting against this fundamental choice in certain situations, such as making the decision, based on resources, to limit the size of the family. Only a fundamental and total reversal to that original commitment will destroy the relationship. In other words, a one hundred and eighty degree turn about would be an actual turning away from the original decision. Small changes still retain the original goal or commitment. Recalling the theological origins of the concept, when the fundamental option involves a complete turning away from God, this is termed a mortal sin. With respect to this context, McBrien (1980, p.955) wrote: "In other words, no single act by itself is sufficient to merit eternal punishment in hell unless that act is of sufficient depth and magnitude to constitute a fundamental repeal of the conversion experience." The difficulty is to determine what individual act is sufficient to constitute a fundamental repeal. The Catholic Church has officially declared that individual sexual actions, like masturbation, are mortal sins in themselves. Some moral theologians in the past have challenged this perspective, and many still do. They claim that too much emphasis is placed on a single action. It ignores the totality of a person's overall commitment to good, or in this case to God. Nonetheless, the official Catholic Church position is to condemn the use of the fundamental option to resolve the morality of individual sexual actions.

None of the Profiled Leaders acted in such a way as to reject totally their commitment to their cause. That is, they never altered this original position with a one hundred and eighty degree change in stance. As noted earlier, each had a weakness but none was sufficient to change the original commitment to their objectives and goals. Not one of these profiled acted contrary to their fundamental option to transform a segment of their society, whether with respect to women suffrage, desegregation, unionization, church reform, nonviolence, or change in government policy. Although it is likely that each person was unaware of the concept of fundamental option, these Profiled Leaders fulfilled its basic tenet of total and consistent commitment in the pursuit of their ultimate objectives or goals.

6. **Civil Disobedience.** The actions of the Profiled Leaders imply that civil disobedience is frequently related to some form of discrimination. The discrimination could be tied to gender (as in the case of Anthony), race (as with King), social class (Chavez), ethnic origin (Gandhi, Mandela), or religion (as evidenced by Pope John's experiences in Turkey, Bulgaria and Greece). The role of discrimination should be qualified to state that discrimination occasioned, rather than caused, civil disobedience. Any causal relationship between discrimination and civil disobedience should be verified. Discrimination may be described as "... an act indicating or implying the inferiority of persons evaluated categorically—e.g., according to race, ethnic origin, religion, or sex—rather than as individuals." (Nuesse, 1967, IV, p.897) Discrimination might be actualized in existing social conventions, civil laws or economic advantage or lack thereof. All the Profiled Leaders who chose civil disobedience did so to rectify what they considered to be an indignity toward humanity. Each had experienced discrimination in one form or other.

Civil disobedience may also occur without discrimination. There was no discrimination based on gender or race towards the dissenters of the Vietnam War, the nuclear power protestors and the automobile speed limit offenders in cities and on expressways. These people willingly broke the civil law. As such, civil law is positive law. It is an ordinance of reason confected and promulgated by legitimate authority for the common good of society. (Aquinas, S.T., I-II, q. 90, a.4) This description raises two important questions about the common good: what is it in a specific situation and who determines what it will be? In times past, some states forbade interracial marriages by law, notably marriages between blacks and whites. The Alabama legislators voted to segregate the races in public facilities and the governor signed this bill into law. This was another application of the "separate but equal" decision of the U.S. Supreme Court. However, related to the Rosa Parks boycott, the Freedom Riders in busses and the Selma March participants, Judge Johnson ruled that the Alabama state law was a violation of the Amendments to the U.S. Constitution that guarantee freedom of speech, equal protection and the right to assembly. The "common good" was thus determined in broader terms than state law permitted. This is a prime example of constitutional law overriding state law and illustrates a hierarchy in positive law.

This hierarchy also exists when there is a conflict of positive law with natural law. A pertinent example is the 1991 U.S. Supreme Court case. It decided on the legality of the "exclusion policy" in companies that prohibited women of child bearing age to work in what were deemed to be more dangerous and higher paying jobs. This was the policy of the Johnson Controls Company, which made batteries. Batteries contain acidic properties that were thought to have the potential to affect the human embryo in a negative way. The Supreme

Court ruled that this employment policy violated the 1964 Civil Rights Act that forbade discrimination based on sex alone. The U.S. Supreme Court uses concrete examples to interpret law and thus to set precedent. The U.S. District Court and the Court of Appeals had previously decided that this company policy in Johnson Controls did not violate the 1964 Civil Rights Act. Writing the majority decision for the U.S. Supreme Court, Justice Sandra Day O'Connor stated that the "exclusion policy" in Johnson Controls was indeed a violation of the Act. This case also decided that children born with handicaps due to the mother working with dangerous chemicals (in this case, lead) could not sue the company. However, some experts think that similar suits in the future will probably favor company exclusion policies. (Carroll, 1996) Currently, more than fifty percent of the states permit children who are handicapped through company negligence to sue the firm.

It is my opinion that the higher law, the natural law, grants the right to life. When this natural right is violated, as in Johnson Controls, through an interpretation of civil law, the higher natural law takes priority and supersedes the human law. To violate the 1964 Civil Rights Act is certainly an act of *civil disobedience*. But the higher law prevails. Furthermore, higher law theory does not have to entertain the issue or question of legislative intent. Positive law does. It asks what did the legislators *really* mean in the context of their decision-making process and what would probably be their intent in today's environment. However, companies who actuate this kind of civil disobedience would have to pay the penalty, according to an interpretation of penal law theory. One interpretation is that if a person breaks the law, even with good intentions, she or he must pay the penalty. Incidentally, the penalty for civil rights violations has generally been monetary.

When power is a "given," as in the cases of the legal power of Judge Johnson, the papal power of Pope John and the economic power of Mr. Feuerstein, there is no need for civil disobedience. The other Profiled Leaders used civil disobedience to augment their power in order to attain equality and justice. Their power was thus increased over various acts of nonviolence, including civil disobedience, directed toward what they considered to be unjust laws on their part. These have proven subsequently to be correct and prudent judgments.

Civil disobedience has its limitations. Traditional ethicists and moral theologians would probably apply penal law theory to justify civil disobedience. Penal law theory can be applied only to civil positive law, not to natural law. Penal law theory has three different components, depending upon the philosophy of the user. First, penal law may be applied when the action is not covered by legislative intent. For example, legislators most likely would not rule in a situation when a driver exceeds a posted speed limit in order to bring a heart attack victim to the nearest hospital. The second kind of penal law would be the willingness to pay the penalty. For example, non-handicapped drivers who park in space reserved for the handicapped should pay the fine. In another example,

Mandela had no problem with his penalty of imprisonment in Robbin Island. The third approach to penal law (not held by all ethicists and moral theologians) is that there is no moral offense as such. The thinking here is that there is no immorality involved in a driver exceeding the speed limit on an empty road in the middle of the night, assuming the driver has not exceeded the state maximum limit of alcohol intake. What can be immoral is an unjust civil law, such as apartheid.

7. Moral Imagination. One popular contemporary ethical concept is moral imagination. Werhane (1999) and others (Moberg and Seabright, 2000) present a challenge to business executives and managers to broaden their perspective to the overall ethical effect of their decisions. Werhane (1999, p.108) describes the concept and concludes that "[M]oral imagination is thus an enabling mechanism for the ongoing process of moral deliberation and moral judgment that is not merely reactive sentimental or absolutist. [It]...anticipates untoward consequences, and projects new practical solutions that take into account a variety points of view and respond to or even create moral demands." Moral imagination thus expands the focus and, more particularly, the perception of different alternatives to a decision. It is practical; it has a limited theoretical dimension.

    Johnson (1993, p. 202) defines moral imagination as "...an ability to imaginatively discern various possibilities for acting within a given situation and to envision the potential help and harm that are likely to result from a given action." Moberg and Seabright (2000, p.185) state that "[O]ur claim is that moral imagination requires decision makers to exhibit flexibility in their use of criteria from all these traditions...[T]he most imaginative option is to use the criterion or criteria that such others' would use for themselves." This approach is difficult if a person follows "role morality," where certain expectations predict human behavior and stability. As a manager, a teacher, or a priest, that person is expected to follow certain predetermined roles. For example, a traditional manager should always consider the bottom line as the only criterion for his or her decisions. A teacher, especially at the grade school or high school levels, has historically been expected to be a role model that favors conformity and conservatism. Many years ago, a person once told me that a "real" priest should be saintly—not human. My response was that it would be impossible to be saintly unless a person is human. Perhaps the sex scandal of Catholic priests in the United States reveals that critics perceive the role of some priests as an abusively human person—a contradiction in terms.

    Carroll (1996, p.136) describes moral imagination as "...the ability to perceive that a web of competing economic relationships is, at the same time, a web of moral and ethical relationships... [this] is extremely challenging because of prevailing methods of evaluating managers." Moral imagination requires that the decision maker attempt to perceive and anticipate a possibly detrimental situation related to those who will be directly and indirectly affected. Werhane (1999, p.13) adds moral reasoning to moral imagination: "...moral reasoning is a crucial statement in management decision making, an element that nevertheless depends on moral imagination as its driving force and on moral standards as its 'bottom line.'" She also singles out Malden Mills, Merck, South Shore Bank and Johnson & Johnson as corporations whose administrators practiced moral imagination. The principals in these corporations exceeded the usual role morality of bottom line supremacy by widening their vision of the possible, or probable, consequences of their decisions upon others. Executives in these firms went beyond the stereotype of "bottom line" decision makers. Werhane (1999) also sees roles as carrying with them certain expectations, rights, duties and norms that might conflict with what is expected of them as moral persons. Indeed, sometimes people become so involved with their roles that their judgments reflect what is expected of them in their roles rather than what is morally acceptable in a particular situation. "Blind obedience" to a person's superior or to "the system" tends to place the fulfillment of a role at a higher level than the expectations of a moral person in society. "Role morality," Werhane (Ibid., p.120) continues, "makes sense only in the context of a broad conception of morality and moral responsibility." The Profiled Leaders rejected the role of "obedient servants" to an unjust system. Even John XXIII and Aaron Feuerstein rejected their roles as an "interim pope" and a "bottom line" executive, respectively. The other persons profiled experienced the deleterious effect of injustice that was triggered by role morality. However, each transformed a segment of society through role imagination. Freeman and Werhane (1994, p.412) reject the "Separation Thesis" wherein the "...idea that economics and ethics are two distinct forms of discourse in describing management and corporate practices." Freeman does not rule out the need for a strong economic base to succeed in actual situations, as Mandela found in his challenge to apartheid and Feuerstein in his recognition of the needs of his employees. In opposition to this, the actions of the top executives at Enron and Arthur Andersen companies exemplify a complete absence of moral imagination.

Werhane (1999) also questions the ability to apply accurately ethical principles to particular cases. She states (p. 42) that "...sometimes there is a *disconnect* between theory and practice." (Italics added.) There is no doubt in my mind from my experience in teaching business ethics to graduate business students that there is a problem of application among lower and mid-level managers. This group frequently has little power to rectify questionable corporate practices. When I interacted with the graduates after they had ten years experience in business, they acknowledge that some of the cases we discussed in class were helpful in resolving their ethical dilemmas. By that time, they had acquired the power to challenge company policies and practices.

A person may intellectually agree with principles as ethically acceptable, but in the practical order he or she may actually chose the very thing these principles condemn. Connery (1952, p.579) makes a distinction between the *antecedent* conscience and the *consequent* conscience. The antecedent conscience sees an act as ethically acceptable, but after the act is completed the consequent conscience realizes that some type of "passion" blocked the true evaluation as good or bad. It can easily be understood how an administrator can block out a more holistic judgment when success or failure of a project is perceived to be more important than its effects on the rights of others. A classic and tragic example involves the decision to launch the *Challenger* spacecraft in spite of warnings from engineers about the danger of using the "O" rings in potentially dangerous and questionable weather conditions. In such situations, behavior is contextual; it is not intellectual or theoretical as it might be discussed in a classroom or articulated in a code of ethics.

The *disconnect* between theory and practice might, and can, be reduced through the use of the virtue of prudence. Prudence is now labeled "practical wisdom." (Gilbey, 1967, XI, p.925) It bridges the gap between theory and practice; that is, it applies general ethical principles to a particular and concrete situation. Prudence is operative: it does not state *what is* but *what must be done*. It *connects* the intellectual to the practical. It is to be found in people of affairs rather than in philosophers. Prudence also has been called "intelligence in action." (Ibid.) It might even be said that prudence in its highest form expands the spirit of freedom against the constraints of positive law. It is, in this limited sense, a reason why civil disobedience can be a prudential act. As detailed previously, some of the Profiled Leaders believed, that nonviolent civil disobedience to an unjust law was, in fact, a prudential act.

To make Transforming Justice operative requires this type of practical wisdom or prudence. Prudence provides the means for attaining its goal. It purviews possible and probable ethical means to its end and orders them to be applied contextually. Justice needs the power of prudence to become effective. Moral imagination may be considered a form of prudence: it perceives all the possible ethical means needed to achieve an end in a particular situation. Like moral imagination, prudence is contextual. It goes beyond role morality. It opens the possibility for a disengaged—not necessarily subjective—application. The term contextual refers to a concrete situation; it does not in and of itself relate to a particular person.

People must have knowledge of a concept before they can need, desire or simply want it. They must know that they have certain rights before they can desire them. The Profiled Leaders illustrate people who chose means to correct the situations in society that did not truthfully respect the rights of human beings. Those being denied their rights first needed to know the truth about their relationships to the broader society. They then could perceive that treatment was unjust. The next goal was to correct the situation. Gandhi sought the highest level of truth when he said that Truth is God. Then he selected means to attain truth. Some of his chosen tactics were efficient, some partially successful, while others were not successful at all. He, as the other Profiled models, frequently employed the prudence of "trial and error." Depending upon the circumstances of time and place, they worked to build up enough power to transform their segment of society. The "spiral theory" mentioned previously, especially in the Gandhi presentation, might be conceptualized as a type of prudence that some of the Profiled Leaders utilized.

Werhane (1999) also challenges the development of principles. She apparently sees principles as coming from some authority, such as a church or the state, without investigating their source. Aristotle and Aquinas make it clear that principles evolve *ut in pluribus* (loosely translated: as in most situations or contexts). Principles are seen as extrapolated from the experiences of society in general. But sometimes these principles result from singular situations. Werhane (1999) acknowledges Donaldson's *universals* or *hypernorms* for multinational corporations. (Donaldson, 1989) These universals are actually principles that Donaldson developed from universal experiences over time. DeGeorge (1995) applies this to situations in which core values differ. He proposed guidelines for multinational companies to improve their relations with host countries. These evolved with experience, rather than appear from "on high." The guidelines are mostly negative in the sense that multinational corporations should not condemn practices in host countries unless they are universally considered to be unethical. These guidelines appear to be examples, perhaps indirectly, of the process of developing universals. The examples evolve into principles.

Although Carroll (1996), Werhane (1999) and others treat moral imagination in terms of business decision-making, there seems to be no reason to limit its application to business. Rights, power and justice are relational and thus operate within the web of social interaction, no matter what the specific situation. Among the Profiled Leaders, only Feuerstein incorporated moral imagination in a business decision. The other persons profiled illustrate some form of moral imagination, each with a unique perception of the concept in their particular contextual situation. Most likely, the individuals involved did not perceive it as such. The moral imagination of Anthony to obtain rights for women clearly differed from Pope John's inspiration to open the windows of the Roman Catholic Church to the world. The particular situations of each Profiled Leaders should not necessarily become categories of moral imagination. Rather, they illustrate how different perceptions and judgments spring from different contexts.

Role morality is also a factor in understanding and appreciating the Transforming Justice of the Profiled Leaders. From Susan B. Anthony to Aaron Feuerstein, none played the role that was expected of them in their unique circumstances. In essence, each was acting out of character. These models were "out of sync" with the norms of prevailing societal expectations. Although role morality is predictable and generally efficient, it can also lessen the freedom that moral reasoning requires for a truly moral decision by constructing an available alternative. It is at this juncture that prudence enters into the decision-making process. Prudence closes the gap between "what is" and "what ought to be"; it selects the most morally appropriate means to close that gap.

These Profiled Leaders illustrate that role reasoning, role morality and moral imagination were intrinsic to their concept and attainment of Transforming Justice. Each was unique. Each was successful, in spite of difficulties. These people were not just outstanding individuals. They became role models for everyone who seeks to transform the injustices of the world into justice and equality.

8. **A Visualization: The Venn Diagram.** A symbol is more than a sign. A sign merely points to something else. On the contrary, a symbol is closer to the thing signified; it is more specific than a sign, although it still has the properties of a sign. A symbol has a special quality and meaning, although frequently this may be limited and ambiguous. A symbol has something of reality in it; that is, it does not refer to something else. Nonetheless, a symbol is limited, in as much as it differs in a way from what is symbolized or, rather, from what gives symbolic form in it. But it is more than it tangibly is and says. (Spleft, 1970)

Throughout history, the circle "always points to the single most vital aspect of life — its ultimate wholeness." (Jaffe, 1964, p.240) On the contrary, "[t]he square...is a symbol of earthbound matter, of the body and reality." (Ibid.)

About 1000 A.D., alchemists in western civilization exalted the mysteries of matter and set them alongside those of the heavenly spirit of Christianity. One of their central symbols was the *quadrature circuli* or the squaring of the circle. *Mandalas,* which are symbolic circles that show the "self" of humans transposed onto a cosmic plane (symbolized in the rose windows of Christian cathedrals), represent wholeness, perfection and other positive qualities. Circles can be found in every religion. Plans of cities (e.g., L'Etoile in Paris and the traffic circles of Washington, D.C.), architecture (especially in many contemporary church structures that are circular rather than the more common cruciform structures of the Renaissance) and art reflect the perfection of the circle and in some degree the "sensory" style which generally depicts a direct reproduction of nature or of the picture-object. (Jaffe, 1964) Justice has been symbolized throughout history as a dyad (two units treated as one), scales (equality), sword and scales (power to cut into two equal parts) and a virgin with stern, straight fixed eyes that neither look to the right nor the left (equality). In the United States the most prevalent symbol is a blindfolded woman holding a balanced scale. Transforming Justice has adapted a symbol from mathematics—the Venn diagram. The Venn diagram uses circles to illustrate various ways of interaction and composition.

This detailed description of symbolism has not been without reason. One of the basic concerns of this book has been the lack of interaction between rights and power in the traditional theories of justice. Granted that related to philosophic thought and dialogue, it is sufficient to determine *what* is just. But the notion of justice as an *active* virtue that persons exercise in their dealings with others goes beyond definition. It touches the realities of everyday life and the realm of person experiences. Life does not separate rights from power. Reflection upon the current separation of rights from power both in theory and in action leads, analogously, to the separation of the "sensory" from the "imaginative" in art and in life. (Jaffe, 1964) The urge to devise a framework of justice that brings out the "wholeness" of its existential being is the underlying rationale for developing a theory of Transforming Justice. Another purpose for developing a theory of Transforming Justice is to suggest a conceptual framework for business and societal ethics and institutional social responsibility that incorporates values, power and virtue. Thus, it is necessary for a conceptual framework to incorporate the quantitative dynamics of power with the qualifying aspects of rights or claims. The symbolic representation of Transforming Justice must capture these basic notions. From Aristotle to Rawls, justice has been and still is viewed as "operative." This view is consistent with the notion of moral virtues that, as stated previously, are geared directly towards operation and not immanent action (like virtue ethics and contemplation) within the person. When perceived as "right plus power," justice acquires an additional dynamism from the infusion of power, which is somewhat akin to energy.

The following Venn diagram illustrates Transforming Justice. This visualization is named after the nineteenth century mathematician and logician John Venn, and consists of three interlocking circles, which are interrelated by some factor. Venn diagrams deal primarily with the testing of a syllogism. A syllogism is an application of logic. A classical syllogism has three different terms: a major, a minor, and a conclusion. As an example of a classical syllogism, a major term would be "Grass is green." A minor term would be "This is grass." From these two terms would flow the conclusion "This is green grass." In the Venn diagram, three overlapping circles contain three different terms. In the case of Transforming Justice, this would be its three components: rights, power and justice. They are independent of each other, but are still related to each other, such as siblings in a family. Just as John is not Tom is not Ann; a right is not power is not justice. But Tom and John and Ann form a unit that is a family. Rights, power and justice can coalesce into something new, Transforming Justice. The point at which the three circles meet is distinct from the circles themselves, although it includes some aspect of each.

As seen in Figure 4.1, Transforming Justice can be illustrated at the intersection the three circles symbolizing rights, power and justice. Each of these is related to the others and contributes to the formation of Transforming Justice. The Venn diagram is a *visualization* of Transforming Justice. It does not attempt to show *causality*. It does not tell us *how* rights, power and justice intersect. The Venn diagram simply illustrates that Transforming Justice is not every kind of rights, power and justice, but only those components that intersect because of some social context.

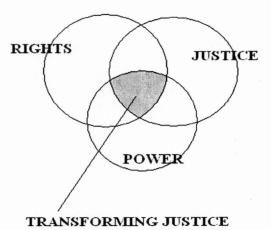

RIGHTS   JUSTICE

POWER

TRANSFORMING JUSTICE

Figure 4.1

As illustrated in this model, not *every* act of rights, power or justice is Transforming Justice. In fact, Transforming Justice is limited to those acts of rights, power and justice that subsequently change the social structure in which it is found. Nonetheless, each of the components keeps its original identity. Thus, not every right is a transforming right. Power is still essentially power but not every power is a component of Transforming Justice. Justice can still be exchange justice, which only indirectly might affect the common good of society. Or it could be contributive justice, distributive justice and social justice, all of which have a direct affect on society. Not every act of Justice is Transforming Justice. Each component contributes in a unique fashion to Transforming Justice. The unique contribution of each might be analogous to the baking of a cake from its ingredients. The cake is something new that has been produced by the combination of ingredients. Butter, flour, eggs, and flavoring in different combinations form various types of cakes: Angel Food, Chocolate Cake or Pound Cake. Another example might be the grilling of meat over a barbecue. A traditional barbecue needs a grill, charcoal and a starter, whether a fluid or gas. In this setting, the starter would be the initial power for a successful grilling. The combination transforms—but does not change the nature—of the meat into something more eatable. (People who prefer the uncooked steak tartare might challenge this example, but in a similar way the addition of onion, raw egg and seasoning does not change the nature of the ground beef.)

There are, nonetheless, limits to Transforming Justice. A person's right to due process at work does not necessarily change the structure of the workplace. Workers can unite in a trade union to bring about change, as in the Darlington case. Nor does the power of an employee's immediate superior change the process of reporting in the whole company. Only the person with authority and power, such as the president or CEO, can legitimately transform this process. The Malden Mills case illustrates the role of authority and power in transforming the role morality of a traditional employer. Employer-employee contracts that include a due process clause are the exception. The paying of a mutually agreed upon just salary is a form of justice (commutative or exchange justice) that rarely affects others in the corporation: a *quid pro quo* contract, like salaries or other forms of recompense, does not often affect others in society. For example, even the huge salaries, stock options and bonuses of CEOs in some corporations do not of themselves directly affect or transform the broader society. However, they *can* affect society at large, as the actions of the Enron Corporation and Arthur Andersen executives exemplify.

Transforming Justice requires structural change that only power can provide. Only those actions of rights, power and justice that bring about structural change in society can be called Transforming Justice. For example, Mandela's use of power, insistence on respect for moral (if not legal) rights and the need for equality (the end or goal of justice) transformed the structure of South Africa. The transformation was to a democratic nation from an apartheid government.

Rights are qualitative; power is quantitative. For example, in a horizontal merger of two firms within the same market, basic rights have not increased; however, power has increased proportionally within that particular market. Theoretically, all firms have equal state and federal rights. Accordingly, the merger or acquisition of companies and, subsequently, an increase in power such as market share, does not by these facts increase their rights. (Conglomerate mergers are an exception, because the acquisition of diverse companies also accrues the rights of these firms.)

A common problem that some individuals might experience (such as non-unionized employees, small business proprietors and homeowners) is a lack of justice while enjoying, in the legal sense, rights. Those who lack justice while enjoying rights might only possess a small amount of power. In situations of this kind an addition of power is required to obtain justice. Power comes from the "outside" in the form of ombudsman, legal procedures, social pressure, the media, or changing conditions of supply and demand. An interesting example of this latter economic power are inventories in times of short supply and heavy demand, such as the demand for knee length overshoes during an unexpected blizzard. The additional power acts somewhat like a catalyst, so that the person or firm receiving the power is "transformed" from lacking justice to "possessing" justice, inasmuch as the person or firm now is capable of exercising justice. The transforming process, while developing within the person or the firm, is recognized by "the other" (the exchange partner) in a social setting. For example, the power of the federal government in civil rights programs reflects this notion of a justice that is transforming. Business firms must acknowledge the rights of minorities and women because of the additional power that they possess through the "outside" action of governmental agencies.

However, power may lead to injustice, and injustice can thus become a "transforming" quality that changes the individual, or, in a structural setting, brings about a structurally unjust social unit. The profiles suggest that each Profiled Leader was challenging an unjust social structure. Power does not necessarily become unjust. Although the rights of an employer and an employee are similar, in the sense that they both can exercise free exchange, the power of the employer and the lack of power of the employees easily reduces the exercise of rights of the employees. The so-called free-exchange employee takes less than is "due" him or her and thus suffers injustice. If the employer permits his or her power to influence other social procedures (such as governmental action, legislation, procedures, etc.), he or she may create a structurally unjust working environment for an employee by increasing the employer's rights through the transforming action of power. In this situation, power increases the scope and limits of rights; the rights of the employer become so broad and inclusive that the individual employee literally becomes "right-less" and powerless. The marginal utility of the employer's power becomes a right.

The previous discussion on the dynamics of Transforming Justice illustrates the adage: at some critical moment, a change in quantity produces a change in quality. The critical moment occurs when the catalyst engages power and rights. The change in quantity, whether by addition or by subtraction, depends upon the amount of power a person possesses. The change in quality means that the persons (individual or corporate) now have the capacity to exercise their rights in such a way that they will obtain justice. In this sense, justice is truly transforming; it grants the power to act *with* one's rights and *for* one's rights. By adding at some critical moment the notion of power, which is quantitative, to the concept of a right, which is qualitative, it can be stated that power produces a change in the *application* of a right. This position might be illustrated by the drinking of alcohol: at some critical moment a person who drinks too many martinis   (quantitative) becomes legally intoxicated (qualitative).

However, the inverse is not necessarily true: a change in quality does not necessarily mean a change in quantity. An academic institution bestows a professional degree such as medicine, law, or theology on students who have met at least the minimum academic and professional standards. The degreed persons thus have been qualified for professional activity. But these persons are not permitted to perform professional duties until they are certified by the state or by a professional body, generally accomplished through testing. With the academic degree, the persons are accorded the status of professionals and may even so indicate in social interchange. They have increased their quality (of life) through a degree. When these persons have been recognized as qualified by their professional body, they then have an increased capacity or power to perform professional duties. The increased power that comes from the outside (the professional society and/or government agency) allows the persons to have that "wholeness" of the professional life. Power adds that dynamism whereby persons can legitimately act within the limitations of their rights as professionals. Otherwise, these persons are qualified, but lack the power to exercise their rights. For example, the late Dr. Armand Hammer, former chairman of Occidental Petroleum, was educated to be a physician, but never exercised his option to practice medicine professionally.

Few would agree that "might makes rights." Nonetheless, power can change the "value added" of rights. Activating rights makes a person more "valuable," at least in the sense that the person now has the capacity to render what is due to another person. That is, the person is now capable of performing an act of justice.

Transforming Justice can be local (*e.g.,* Feuerstein and Malden Mills in a relatively small city). Transforming Justice can also be applied to broader geographic areas such as state, region or national impact as the Mandela example demonstrates. U.S. Supreme Court decisions affect the entire nation. Acquisitions and mergers can transform local, regional, national and even international markets. But these changes are not of their nature directly related to justice that transforms. Acquisitions, mergers and reorganization are not ordinarily made for the purpose of justice, but for related competition, especially in global competition. The mergers of telephone companies with cable corporations have generally been made for competitive reasons. Does this mean that Transforming Justice (of its nature) *cannot* be achieved in acquisitions, mergers and reorganizations? Not at all, as Transforming Justice may include these instances when they impact individuals, primarily employees and shareholders, local communities or national interests in a manner that recognizes and respects their rights, both legal and ethical. In so doing, Transforming Justice requires a structural social change, as exemplified by the Profiled Leaders. When two firms decide to merge in the same market, such as Ameritech and SBC in the telephone industry, the merger is called "horizontal." The rights of SBC remain the same, but they have been extended to include the Mid-Western States. However, the union of these two corporations has increased market share and thus the merger has formed a more powerful company. This union has quantitatively increased but remains the same qualitatively. It may or may not have a social impact. It is essentially a contract to gain more power in an economy that is becoming more global. Acquisitions and mergers can transform local, regional, national and international economies and lifestyles. When Chrysler closed, without previous notice or warning, their recently acquired American Motors plant in Kenosha, Wisconsin, in 1986, the corporation created economic chaos in the city, a high unemployment rate

(Chrysler was the largest employer) and low morale throughout the region. (McMahon, 1999)   The closing was certainly transforming, but hardly an exercise of justice. The situation also demonstrated a lack of moral imagination on the part of the top executives.

The Venn diagram can be applied to the situation of each of the Profiled Leaders. Each person has her or his particular rights, power and justice. Each of these may be placed in respective circles. Each will have a unique form or type of Transforming Justice. None is more ethical or moral than the others. The *legal* Transforming Justice of Judge Frank Johnson is no more ethical than the *social* Transforming Justice of Dr. Martin Luther King, Jr.   Each man transformed society in his own particular way.   The Venn diagram thus illustrates both the similarities and the differences of the Profiled Leaders as a visualization of Transforming Justice.

9. Liberation Theology. A colleague of mine from Loyola University Chicago and her husband, a prominent lawyer in Chicago, invited me to a celebratory dinner at an internationally recognized restaurant in Chicago. During the course of our dinner, the conversation turned to my book on Transforming Justice. The lawyer asked me what did Transforming Justice mean and what was its principal theme.   When I stated that the basic definition was rights plus power equal justice, I emphasized the role of power in obtaining and in exercising rights. Without any hesitation, he responded that this concept sounded like "Liberation Theology," a position developed a number of years ago in Latin America, primarily by Catholic theologians. Liberation Theology emphasized the role of power in changing oppressive conditions. I was astounded. I had never made the connection. It became clear to me that the concept Transforming Justice, as presented in the preceding sections, had to be reviewed in terms of Liberation Theology.   I now have to answer the question the lawyer raised: "Is Transforming Justice the same as Liberation Theology?"

Liberation Theology refers to any theological movement that criticizes and challenges oppression.   Liberation is integral to the theological concept itself.   It focuses on inequality among persons in society and makes liberation *from* political, economic, and even theological oppression its goal.   It rejects development *of* the categories that increase inequality, such as wealth and power. It denies the position that development of wealth and power has a "trickle down" effect to the poor and the powerless. *Development* of its nature means expansion of "what is."   Latin American Liberation Theology primarily denounces the socio-political domination of development. This domination has had widespread negative effects on the quality of life of its citizens.   Freedom of speech, economic stability and adequate education were almost nonexistent for the majority populations in Latin America. Liberation Theology also rejects the almost absolute power of the "haves" over the "have-nots." However, Liberation Theology in the United States has a different perspective, as exemplified by the desegregation required in black theology and the discrimination condemned in feminist theology.

Schussler-Fiorenza (1981) states that all Liberation Theologies share a common theological methodology. This common methodology brings awareness of the sociological underpinnings of theology, the relation between theory and *praxis* (practice), and a thorough investigation of its social, political, and cultural environment. Three basic traits constitute the common methodology of all Liberation Theologies: first, the starting point which assesses the existing context and assumptions; secondly, reflection on religious tradition; and, thirdly, a reconstructive task for attaining equality. These are detailed in the following sections.

(a) Starting Point

The *starting point* of all types of Liberation Theology is an analysis of the actual socio-political situation and the uncovering of any questionable discrimination, alienation, and oppression within the existing environment. It censures theories that reinforce development and do not attempt to correct exploitation. Liberalism, and particularly the economic liberalism of such scholars as Milton Friedman of the Hoover Institute and business executives such as Jack Welch of General Electric, stresses *development* at the expense of other values, such as conservation measures to protect the environment. The "trickle down effect" of development that is supposed to help the needy has yet to be proven empirically. As stated above, development means that an entity expands; it becomes fuller and larger without change in its basic structure, whether social, political, or religious. In this sense, the wealthy and the powerful become wealthier and more powerful, while the poor and the less powerful become less so, perhaps even powerless. Thus, development becomes a tool for subjugation, oppression and domination. On the contrary, the Liberation Theologies demand freedom from all oppressive policies and practices that by their nature do not respect the dignity of the person. By analysis of the concrete situation, all Liberation Theologies undertake to demonstrate not only the existence of discrimination or oppression, but also their economic and cultural causes. Indeed, in each Liberation Theology, the present experience and analysis of injustice has led to a critique of the past, an erg when cultural and religious traditions permitted or even encouraged domination in Latin America and in the United States. Liberation Theology proponents view human existence as marked by economic conflict, disparity and oppression and the suffering these generate. This is the milieu in which liberationists operate; this is their *starting point*.

(b) Pragmatic Approaches

The next step is to find ways to correct this unbalance. McBrien (1980, p.133) calls these theologians, and others of similar convictions, "philosophical pragmatists." That is, they observe the oppressive situation and find practical ways to remove it. Pragmatists, such as John Dewey, Charles Darwin and Karl Marx, call for an actual change in reality; for them and for other pragmatists it is not enough to theorize about what should be done. Theorizing might be acceptable in a classroom or at a conference of professionals. But without practical consequences, they would insist that a concept such as Liberation Theology has no real meaning.

Some critics might even consider Liberation Theology to be theological consequentialism. From this viewpoint only the effects, not the means, would be considered the production of a remedy for the poor and the powerless. From another perspective, Liberation Theology can be perceived as a type of Utilitarianism, or the Social Good theory of justice (as discussed above), which postulates that ethics is reduced to the greatest good for the greatest number. For Liberation Theologians, the greatest good would refer to liberation from oppression and the greatest number would relate to the poor and the powerless. From an ethical perspective, a problem arises if there are no underlying philosophical principles independent of practical content, there can be no moral norms by which a person can determine what is morally good. In other words, pragmatism, and perhaps even consequentialism, ultimately leads to ethical relativism. (The theory of pragmatism was discussed more thoroughly in the section on justice.) A criticism of Liberation Theology is that it, too, might foster ethical relativism by its insistence on bringing change to the concrete situation in ways that do not incorporate, or may even ignore, ethical philosophical and metaphysical principles. "Power"—economic, political, social, moral—is the engine that brings about the necessary changes for liberation from oppression.

McBrien (1980, p.192) makes an interesting comparison when he associates the power tactics of Martin Luther King, Jr. with those of the Latin American liberation theologians: "Connected with the sense of human solidarity is...*compassionate protest*...It is the experience of those who become deeply disturbed by the misery in life, who are burdened by the presence of injustice, exploitation, and war...Martin Luther King, Jr....personifies this experience. And, so, too, perhaps do some of the *theologians of liberation* in Latin America, such as Gustavo Gutierrez of Peru, Juan Luis Secundo of Uruguay, and Hugo Assman of Brazil." (Italics in original.) Leonardo Boff of Brazil also requires a change in reality. From his perspective, the justice of Jesus, the messianic king, would definitively reject wealth and dominative power.

With the exception of Judge Frank Johnson, John XXIII, and Aaron Feuerstein, the other Profiled Leaders had their *starting point* with an analysis of a concrete socio-political situation. The analysis involved uncovering of alienation and oppression within such a context. For example, Pope John XXIII acknowledged that the Roman Catholic Church did not sufficiently recognize the basic rights of other religions to worship God as they deemed appropriate. That was his starting point—a clearly observable fact, but not a socio-political situation. It could also be argued persuasively, that Johnson and Feuerstein acted from a perspective of the concrete.   Johnson recognized an abuse of constitutional law in the Alabama state segregation laws, while Feuerstein perceived the threat of a devastating economic situation on his employees and on the city of Lawrence, Massachusetts. However, as such, they did not personally suffer oppression *before* their decisions, as the other Profiled Leaders did. Nonetheless, Johnson was granted police protection for several years after his landmark decisions.   In this case, his personal oppression came *after* his decisions wherein he determined the constitutional rights of the protestors. Thus, the *starting point* of at least five of the eight Profiles of Transforming Justice and that of the theologians of Liberation Theology were similar: all perceived some type of socio-political oppression against the powerless.

(c) Religious Tradition and Liberation Theology

The second trait in Liberation Theology is a reflection on religious tradition in relation to contemporary oppression. Much of the Latin American Liberation Theology examines how the Roman Catholic Church's mission has been understood both in the distinct but separate roles of clergy and laity, and in the separation between its salvific function from its concern for justice in the world. Faith must be understood as a transforming incorporation of the Word of God, expressed in the cries of the oppressed. For Christians the reference point is the story of the life of Jesus. Feminist theology points out that the masculine language and symbols in organized religion have become institutionalized. Black theology claims that blackness, whiteness, and their separation in the Church have led to oppression, both historically and currently. Thus, in each form of Liberation Theology, the present experience of perceived injustice has led to a critique not only of the present, but also of the past from which cultural and religious traditions have been constructed. (Schussler-Fiorenza, 1981) Those profiled will be reviewed in terms of their religious contribution to Transforming Justice in the third common trait: Transforming Justice is *per se* an ethical concept that may incorporate religious doctrine, practice, and tradition, but it does not necessarily require such doctrine.

(d) Retrieval and Reinterpretation

The third common trait that the three Liberation Theologies propose is the need for retrieval and reinterpretation of religious practices. For example, proponents of this conceptualization would state that sin should be viewed in terms of socio-political oppression, inequality of women's rights, and racial suppression. They would say that the concept of sin should not concentrate on some human fault of an *individual.* In the context of Liberation Theology, sin is primarily *social.*   It is related to any institutional oppression, whether political or corporate, that dehumanizes an individual.

Unlike Liberation Theology that has a religious and biblical foundation, Transforming Justice, as such, has an ethical base in natural law for retrieval and reinterpretation.   The concept does not necessarily have a religious or theological underpinning.   Nonetheless, recognized philosophers and theologians like Pieper (1965), Fuchs (1965), Maritain (1949), Haring (1961), and more recently, editors Stackhouse and McCann (1995), generally hold the view that natural law ultimately depends upon a biblical dimension for its full understanding.   The profiles of John XXIII, King, Chavez and Feuerstein demonstrate that these individuals incorporated a religious dimension into their pursuit of justice.   Gandhi also had deep religious convictions that affected his search for Truth.   On the other hand, it was the tenets of secular socio-political liberation, rather than the biblical mandates of Liberation Theology, that influenced the perception of justice by Mandela and Anthony.

The third methodological trait in all three types of Liberation Theology includes a twofold constructive task of retrieval and reinterpretation.   In other words, this approach inevitably asks what should be done to restructure, and what is the foundation for this restructuring of the socio-political liberating process.   A number of the Latin American proponents of Liberation Theology, including Gutierrez, target the capitalism of the U.S. multinational corporation as a means for the reconstruction of Third World countries.   Surprisingly, at a much later date, Gutierrez admitted, very theoretically, that if evidence showed that capitalism actually and effectively relieved poverty, there could be a capitalist Liberation Theology. (Sherman, 1990)   Nonetheless, the tenets of Marxism pervade Liberation Theology.   This approach stands for the revival of socialism in Latin America.   The atheism, philosophical materialism and proposed violence in the class struggle indigenous to Marxism do not reflect a truly *Christian* Liberation Theology.   Nonetheless, a leading Latin American Liberation Theology advocate, Bishop Helder Camara of Olinda-Recife, Brazil, has been quoted as saying that the Roman Catholic Church must do with Marx today what Thomas Aquinas did with Aristotle in medieval times. (Benne, 1981) This is a telling call to action, since some theologians jokingly say that Aquinas "baptized" Aristotle!

As stated previously, Transforming Justice is an application of natural law.   Natural law acknowledges the basic right of a person to own property. However, this right is not absolute.   Natural law also requires that a person with an excessive accumulation of material goods share these goods with those less fortunate.   (This obligation was discussed above in the section on distributive justice.)   Social justice requires a person to contribute to the common good, no matter how the "common good" is defined or concretized.   On the one hand, these mandates to share with the less fortunate go far beyond the tenets of economic liberalism with its individualistic interpretation of sharing.   On the other hand, they do not incorporate the strictly materialistic tenets of Marxism, either as a basic socialism or as its more expansive application in communism.

(e) **The Profiled Leaders and Liberation Theology**

The Profiled Leaders perceived their mission in terms of a truly democratic society. Although each experienced first hand the pitfalls of this system, in his or her own way had attempted to bring about change in a nonviolent, progressive manner. As stated above, Liberation Theology incorporates the need for change from *development,* in which the structure stays the same, but progress expands its application to *liberation,* which requires radical change in structure. That is, it rejects capitalism and adopts a form of Marxism. However, Gutierrez suggests that there is, at least in theory, a form of capitalism that could possibly provide "a preferential option for the poor."

None of those profiled rejected capitalism as the base of their activities. Indeed, Mandela demonstrated the effectiveness of capitalism. The withdrawal from South Africa of investments and businesses by foreign countries and banks brought about economic pressure that finally broke down the barriers of apartheid. The approach of these Profiled Leaders was not to replace capitalism with Marxism, but to correct the socio-political structures that denied or reduced the human dignity of the person. To that end, Johnson employed legal power and Feuerstein used economic power of a democratic society to bring about change. They did not use their power to change the structure of society from a democratic society to a state-owned, socialistic nation. They rejected governmental oppression, as do the Liberation Theologians. These men and woman used their power to bring about a change in traditional legal and economic *applications* ultimately acceptable in a democratic society. Consequently, Transforming Justice is not simply a more sophisticated *genre* of Liberation Justice.

Mandela employed a Liberation *Ethic,* not a Liberation *Theology,* in restructuring South Africa. Mandela was more intent in establishing a democracy wherein all people were treated equal under the law than he was in demonstrating a Christian theology that rejects oppression. Liberation Theology does not eliminate *violence,* however, as a means of obtaining equality. As stated previously, Mandela denounced terrorism as a means to obtain a democratic government. He did not, however, reject the violence of guerilla warfare. As a consequence of the economic and political changes that became apparent, white South Africaners feared that Mandela would incorporate communism into the restructuring of the nation. It was believed during the transition that South Africa could become a communist state under Mandela. This fear stemmed from the awareness that the Russians offered foreign aid to his cause and that Fidel Castro, Mandela's role model, used guerilla warfare to overcome a repressive Cuban government. Nonetheless, Mandela rejected communism and established a democracy that provided constitutional equality for all citizens. Thus, the restructuring proposed by Liberation Theology differs appreciably from the change that Transforming Justice prescribes and the process that Mandela followed.

The concepts of Transforming Justice and Liberation Theology are similar in certain aspects, especially related to their starting points. But it should be noted that "similarity" is not "identity." For example, the nonviolence of Cesar Chavez was similar to the nonviolence of Martin Luther King, Jr. Both challenged the civil law that repressed their basic human and constitutional rights as their starting points. But the right to unionize, of which Chavez was a strong proponent, differed appreciably from the right to desegregated public transportation that was King's cause. These two illustrations are similar in that they both employed nonviolence. Indeed, both used the same means of boycotts, sit-ins and marches to obtain their immediate end. But their ends differed. The starting points in Liberation Theology and Transforming Justice are similar: both criticize the existing repressive socio-political environment and condemn it. Although their starting points are similar, they are not identical. On the one hand, Martin Luther King, Jr. in the United States perceived segregation and other signs of inequality as a form of oppression and domination. On the other hand, the Latin American Liberation Theologians were concerned with the repressive institutionalized inequality of wealth and power.

Another similarity is obvious. Both theories require *praxis*, that is, some form of action, rather than merely the analysis and evaluation of a theory. Both ideologies are concerned with power and rights. However, Transforming Justice is not necessarily restricted to the poor, the powerless and the oppressed. The Transforming Justice of Feuerstein towards his employees, who were neither "poor" nor oppressed, differs appreciably from the Liberation Theology of the Latin Americans, which deals exclusively with an oppressed underclass. The power of Transforming Justice also differs from Liberation Theology in that the first incorporates a variety of types of power (economic, legal, social, and moral), while the second stresses social and political power. Liberation Theology is also concerned with the lack of economic power among the general population. Additionally, the purposeful acts of nonviolence of most of our Profiled Leaders exhibiting Transforming Justice stands in contradistinction to the permissible violence in Liberation Theology.

The answer to the question as to whether Transforming Justice is a form of Liberation Theology is a definite and resounding "No." As explained above, the two ideologies share similarities, but lack identity.

(f) High Context and Low Context Cultures

Each of the Profiled Leaders operated within a social context. This context can be classified along a continuum as "high" to "low" as it relates to cultural analysis. Edward Hall (1976) explored this conceptualization of culture. High context requires the Profiled Leader to relate to the others in a warm, friendly manner of experiential trust. A person has to feel "comfortable" with the other person before she or he will submit to a commitment. The Japanese belong to one of the most high context cultures in the world. Gifts have to be given and meals and social activities have to be shared. "Trust" has to be developed. This trust must be built before business contracts are agreed upon. American businessmen and women find this high context difficult to comprehend—and to practice. Gandhi, in India, and John XXIII, especially related to the Catholic Church in Bulgaria, Turkey and Greece, operated in a high context society.

Most of the Profiled Leaders in this book adhere to the low context culture typical of Western Europe and North America. A low context society does not depend upon trusting social relationships. It is rather based upon oral or, preferably, written contractual agreements. It is an application of legal justice and a form of commutative justice. The status, family relationship and societal role of the person do not enter into the agreement. Anthony, King, Johnson and Feuerstein, and perhaps Mandela operated in a low context society. It might be argued that Chavez operated at first in a high context role because of his close interaction with his followers and the communities in which he operated.

The difference between a high context and a low context culture may be defined within geographical boundaries. Japan, the Pacific Rim and the Middle Eastern nations operate within a high context environment. As a person travels north, the context gradually shifts from high to low context, with Northern Europe and England as the low context cultures. The United States, Canada and Australia follow English customs and laws and are consequently low context. Business people in a low context environment have difficulty in adjusting to a high context society, even though the vast majority of the world's population is high context. The opposite is also true. Africa, with its tribes, and South America, with its "patron" system, generally operate within a high context system.

Gandhi and Mandela are two Profiled Leaders who were born into a high context society, but had to operate in a low context environment. The British Establishment in India and the apartheid government of South Africa operated in a low context environment within a high context society of tribes and castes. Each Profiled Leader ultimately attained his goals through adjustment and compromising that incorporated to some degree both high and low context practices. This different cultural orientation suggests two things. First, what is perceived as an ethical imperative in a low context society may not even be an ethical dimension in a high context society. For example, the equality of women with men is an issue in low context societies, whereas high context societies see gender roles as a fact of societal structures. The opposite is also true: low context business persons may lose patience during the long process of socialization and trust-building before a contractual agreement is reached in a high context society. In another example, the practice we would term "bribery" in Western Civilization is common in the form of "gifting" in a high context society . My students from the Pacific Rim countries were amused when I explained the U.S. Corrupt Practices Act. Some said that their families could not stay in business if they did not pay bribes, conceptualized as "gifts," to government officials.

An important point related to cultural context is that the differences in high context and low context societies might have some bearing upon the weaknesses that were discussed previously. It is conceivable that an action that is judged to be a weakness in a low context society may be a powerful tool for change in a high context environment. Civil disobedience might be classified as such. An example might illustrate this difference. In Rome, Italy, outside one of the gates in the ancient wall surrounding the city are two statues. One is St. Peter with his finger pointing to a book resting on his arm. The other statue is that of St. Paul who has his arm extended and finger pointing to the outside. The wags claim that what this really means is that we make the laws here in Rome but that you keep them out there! In a relatively high context society, such as Italy, the interpretation and understanding of such non-verbal subtlety may not be an exaggeration.

Liberation Theology was developed in the high context society of South America. Most of the Profiled Leaders acted within a low context society. Regardless, the high context of Liberation Theology cannot easily be applied to the low context of those profiled in Transforming Justice. Nonetheless, Gandhi and Mandela were able to transcend these differences.

C. Conclusions

As seen from the discussion throughout this book, Transforming Justice has many facets. As the profiles illustrated, not one kind of right, power, or justice predominates. What is common among the Profiled Leaders is that there is a social dimension in all their situations. It is now possible to bring these components together to show that the different Profiled Leaders suggest various ways of understanding Transforming Justice. The following four principles emerge from the discussion explicated in this book:

1. **Not all rights, power and justice are applicable to Transforming Justice.** Only the rights, power and justice that *intersect* in the Venn diagram illustrated above contribute to Transforming Justice. As stated above, the Venn diagram is a *visualization* of Transforming Justice. It does not attempt to show *causality*. To be called Transforming Justice, all rights, all power and all justice have to be perceived within a social context, as stated above. When these *three* components intersect, Transforming Justice exists. It could happen that only rights and power intersect. This would be a form of exchange justice. For example, a customer has certain rights but needs power from the outside to obtain justice from the seller. This could be the power of the media, such as the "Trouble Shooters" of Chicago's CBS Channel 2. They help individuals solve a specific problem, but are unlikely to have little impact on the larger society. Even class action suits provide a type of power to implement rights so the *individuals* of the class action receive justice. This is also exchange justice. It

does not directly affect society at large. Consequently, it is not Transforming Justice. Thus, not all rights produce Transforming Justice. Another example is that the right to a just settlement in the sale of a house does not of itself relate to Transforming Justice. It also exemplifies exchange or commutative justice.

Not all power is an application of Transforming Justice. The judicial power of Judge Frank Johnson permitted Martin Luther King, Jr. the opportunity to dissent against unjust government laws. These nonviolent actions transformed the justice of a whole segment of society. The judicial power of a district court judge is limited and generally has no widespread societal impact. For example, a judicial decision on the obligation of a tenant to pay her rent in winter when the landlord is not providing adequate heat affects the tenant, but has little effect on society. Judicial power of this kind is used to determine the rights and obligations of the contracting parties; it relates to commutative or exchange justice. Justice attained in a traffic court when an offender pays a fine is not Transforming Justice. Not paying a fine might have some effect on society if the practice becomes widespread or cumulative. These examples of intersecting rights and power show that *some* type of justice may be attained, but it is not Transforming Justice. Aaron Feuerstein's commitment to his employees and the city of Lawrence, Massachusetts, was the exception; it had widespread social implications. It was indeed an example of distributive Transforming Justice. Thus, not all rights, powers and justices are applicable to Transforming Justice.

    2.   Transforming Justice brings about direct change in society. Most of the Profiled Leaders brought about social change that ultimately had legal consequences. Examples cited in the profiles begin with Susan B. Anthony's effort to obtain voting rights for women and conclude with Nelson Mandela's protests that brought about a very basic change in the structure and functioning of government. Social change frequently precedes legislation, since laws are passed only after legislators and society become aware of injustice. The Profiled Leaders engaged in social activities that at least occasioned, if not caused, favorable legislation for their causes.

    3.   Transforming Justice is most often a specification of distributive, contributive or social justice. This can also include specific types of commutative, or exchange, justice. Some say that distributive justice lies only with the state. They would call Feuerstein's commitment to his employees a type of commutative justice, or even philanthropy. I prefer to see his action as distributive justice: he is distributing his personal wealth to his employees.

    4.   The Profiles illustrate that each of the Profiled Leaders employed different approaches as well as specific means to attain Transforming Justice. The following table summarizes each Profiled Leader's application of rights, power and justice in attaining Transforming Justice.

Table 4.1

Person	Rights	Power	Transforming Justice
Susan B. Anthony	Civil Equality	Legislative	Legal
Mahatma Gandhi	Human	Moral	Contributive
Judge Frank Johnson	Bill of Rights	Judicial	Legal
Martin Luther King, Jr.	Bill of Rights	Nonviolent	Social
Pope John XXIII	Canonical	Papal	Ecumenical
Cesar Chavez	Civil	Social	Exchange
Nelson Mandela	Human	Political	Interracial
Aaron Feuerstein	Property	Economic	Distributive

Various readers of this book might perceive these conceptualizations of rights, power and justice differently. They may challenge these conclusions, especially in the table above. I enthusiastically endorse such criticism, as the discussion of the concept of Transforming Justice can only lead to its better understanding, clarification, and hopefully, application. The concept of Transforming Justice developed in this book is vital and dynamic. Rather than gather dust on someone's bookcase, my dream is that it continues to surface in examples of social change for the common good or for those whose voices are muted by prejudice or injustice in any form.

BIBLIOGRAPHY

Abela, A. 2001. "Profit and More: Catholic Social Teaching and the Purpose of the Firm." *Journal of Business Ethics.* Vol.31. Pp.107-116.

Abruzzese, J. 2001. "Synod of Bishops, Special Assembly for America." *New Catholic Encyclopedia.* Washington, D.C.: Gale Group/The Catholic University of America. Pp. 170-171.

Ackerman, R. 1975. *The Social Challenge to Business.* Cambridge, Massachusetts: Harvard University Press.

Adler, M. 1978. *Aristotle for Everybody: Difficult Thought Made Easy.* New York: Macmillan.

----- 1981. *Six Great Ideas.* New York: Macmillan.

Alden, C. 1996. *Apartheid's Last Stand: The Rise and Fall of South African Security State.* London: Macmillan.

Alejandro, R. 1998. *The Limits of Rawlsian Justice.* Baltimore: The Johns Hopkins University Press.

Ambler, R. 1989. "Gandhi's Concept of Truth." *Gandhi's Significance Today.* Hick, J. and Hempel, L., eds. New York: St. Martin's Press. Pp. 90-108.

Anderson, A. 1997. *Universal Justice: A Dialectical Approach.* Atlanta: Rodopi.

Anthony, K. 1954. *Susan B. Anthony: Her Personal History and Her Era.* Garden City, New Jersey: Doubleday.

Aquinas, T. 1947. *Summa Theologica.* English Dominican Province, trans. New York: Benziger Brothers.

Aristotle. 1976. *The Ethics of Aristotle: The Nicomachian Ethics.* Thomson, J., trans. New York: Penquin.

Ascenzi, J. 2000. "Latinos Back Move By California Legislature for Cesar Chavez Holiday." Knight-Ridder/Tribune Business News. p ITEM00047030.

Bailey, J. 1997. *Utilitarianism, Institutions and Justice.* New York: Oxford University Press.

Bardacke, F. 1993. "Cesar's Ghost: Decline and Fall of the U.F.W." *The Nation.*Vol. 257. No. 4. Pp. 130-136.

Barry, K. 1988. *Susan B. Anthony: Biography of A Single Feminist.* New York: New York University Press.

Bass, J. 1993. *Taming the Storm: The Life and Times of Judge Frank Johnson, Jr., and The South's Fight over Civil Rights.* New York: Doubleday.

Baumhart, R. 1969. *An Honest Profit: What Businessmen Say About Ethics in Business.* New York: Holt, Rinehart and Winston.

Bayles, M., ed. 1968. *Contemporary Utilitarianism.* Garden City, New York: Doubleday.

Beard, M. 1938. A History of Business: From Babylon to the Monopolist, Vol. 1. Ann Arbor, Michigan: The University of Michigan Press.

----- 1963. *A History of Business: From the Monopolists to the Organization Man.* Vol. 2. Ann Arbor, Michigan: The University of Michigan Press.

Becker, L. 1983. "Individual Rights." *Justice for All.* Regan, T and VanDeVeer, D., eds. Totowa, New Jersey: Roman & Allanheld. Pp. 197-214.

Bedau, H. 1971. "Radical Egalitarianism." *Justice and Equality.* Brody, B., ed. Englewood Cliffs, New Jersey: Prentice-Hall, Inc. Pp. 168-180.

Benn, S. 1971. "Egalitarianism and the Equal Consideration of Interests." *Justice and Equality.* Brody, B., ed. Englewood Cliffs, New Jersey: Prentice-Hall, Inc. Pp. 152-167.

Bennett, J. 1998. Book Review: *Toward Justice and Virtue: A Constructive Account Of Practical Reason.* By O'Neill, O. *Review of Metaphysics.* Vol. 5. Pp. 707-708.

Benson, M. 1994. *Nelson Mandela: The Man and the Movement.* London: Penguin.

Bentham, J. 1970. *An Introduction to the Principles of Moral and Legislation.* (1789) Burns, J. and Hart, H., eds. London: Athlone.

Bernadin, J. 1986. "Forward." *Vatican II Revisited.* Stacpoole, A., ed. Minneapolis: Winston. Pp. xi-xv.

Berle, A. 1959. *Power Without Property: A New Development in American Political*

Economy. New York: Harcourt, Brace & World.

----- 1967 and Means, G. *The Modern Corporation and Private Property.* Rev. ed. New York: Harcourt, Brace & World.

----- 1969. *Power.* New York: Harcourt, Brace & World.

Berry, M. 1994. *Black Resistance, White Law: A History of Constitutional Racism in America.* New York: Viking.

Biddle, F. 1961. *Justice Holmes, Natural Law, and the Supreme Court.* New York: Macmillan.

Bird, O. 1967. *The Idea of Justice.* New York: Frederick A. Praeger.

Boatright, J. 1999. *Ethics and the Conduct of Business.* Third Edition. Upper Saddle River, New Jersey: Prentice-Hall.

Bockle, F. and Pohier, J., eds. 1973. *Power and the Word of God.* New York: Herder and Herder.

Brian, B. 1971. "Reflections on 'Justice as Fairness.'" *Justice and Equality.* Brody, B., ed. Englewood Cliffs, New Jersey: Prentice-Hall.

Brody, B., ed. 1971. *Justice and Equality.* Englewood Cliffs, New Jersey: Prentice-Hall.

Brown v. Board of Education of Topeka, Kansas. 1954. 347 U.S. 483.

Brunner, E. 1945. *Justice and the Social Order.* New York: Harper and Harper.

Buchanan, A. 1987. "Justice and Charity." *Ethics.* Vol. 97. Pp. 558-575.

Buechler, S. 1990. *Women's Movements in the United States: Woman Suffrage, Equal Rights and Beyond.* New Brunswick, New Jersey: Rutgers University Press.

Cahill, T. 2002. *Pope John XXIII.* New York: Viking Penguin.

Can, E. 1949. *The Sense of Injustice.* New York: New York University Press.

Canton, J. 2001. Book Review: *Ties That Bind.* Donaldson, T. and Dundee, T. 1999. *Business and Society.* Vol. 40. Pp. 220-225.

Campbell, T. 1988. *Justice.* London: Macmillan.

Capovilla, L. 1986. "Reflections on the Twentieth Anniversary." *Vatican II Revisited.* Stackpoole, A., ed. Minneapolis: Winston. Pp. 110-128.

Carroll, A. 1996. *Business & Society: Ethics and Stakeholder Management.* 3rd. ed. Cincinnati: South –Western.

Carter, A. 1995. *Mahatma Gandhi: A Selected Bibliography.* Westport, Connecticut: Greenwood.

Cascardi, A., ed. 1987. *Literature and the Question of Philosophy.* Baltimore: The Johns Hopkins University Press.

Cavanagh, G. 1976. *American Values in Transition.* Englewood Cliff, New Jersey: Prentice-Hall.

Chayes, A. 1976. "The Role of the Judge in Public Law Litigation." *Harvard Law Review.* Vol. 89. Pp. 121-136.

Chelton, K. and Orlande, M. "A New Social Contract for the American Worker." *Business and Society Review.* No. 96. Pp. 23-26.

Chenu, —D. 1986. "A Council for All Peoples." *Vatican II Revisited.* Stackpoole, A., ed. Minneapolis: Winston. Pp. 19-23.

Chaplin, M. 1986. "Pope and Journalist." *Gregorianum.* Vol. 67. Pp. 517-531.

Christiansen, D. 1984. "On Relative Equality: Catholic Egalitarianism After Vatican II." *Theological Studies.* Vol. 45. Pp. 651-675.

Ciulla, J. 1998. "Imagination, Fantasy, Wishful Thinking and Truth." The Ruffin Series. Special Issue #1. *Business Ethics Quarterly.* Pp. 99-107.

Clark, J. 1966. *Religion and Moral Standards of American Businessmen.* Cincinnati: South-Western.

Cochran, T. 1957. *The American Business System: A Historical Perspective 1900-1950.* New York: Harper & Row.

Cohen, D. 1998. "Moral Imagination in Organizational Problem-Solving: An Institutional Perspective." The Ruffin Series. Special Issue #1. *Business Ethics Quarterly.* Pp. 123-147.

Collins, D. 1996. *Farm Workers' Friend: The Story of Cesar Chavez.* Minneapolis: Carolschoda.

Congar, Y. 1986. "Moving Towards a Pilgrim Church." *Vatican II Revisited.* Stackpoole, A., ed. Minneapolis: Winston. Pp. 129-152.

----- 1986. "A Last Look at the Council." *Vatican II Revisited.* Stackpoole, A., ed. Minneapolis: Winston. Pp. 337-358.

Connery, J. 1952. "Prudence and Morality." *Theological Studies.* Vol. 13. Pp. 564-582.

Covell, C. 1992. *The Defense of Natural Law.* New York: St. Martin's Press.

Cox, H. 1967. "Power." *Dictionary of Christian Ethics.* Macquarre, J., ed. Philadelphia: Westminster. P. 265.

Cranston, M. 1973. *What Are Human Rights?* London: Bodley.

Curran, C. 1967. "Civil Law, Moral Obligation of." *New Catholic Encyclopedia.* Washington, D.C.: Catholic University of America. Vol. III. Pp. 893-897.

Dahl, R. 1970. *After the Revolution: Authority in a Good Society.* New Haven: Yale University Press.

Dasgupta, S. 1989. "The Core of Gandhi's Social and Economic Thought." *Gandhi's Significance Today.* Hick, J. and Hempel, L, eds. New York: St. Martin's Press. Pp. 189-202.

Davis, K. and Blomstrom, R. 1971. *Business, Society and Environment: Social Power and Social Response.* 2nd ed. New York: McGraw-Hill.

Del Vecchio, G. 1956. *Justice: An Historical and Philosophical Essay.* Campbell, A., ed. Edinburgh: Edinburgh University Press.

Donaldson, T. 1989. *The Ethics of International Business.* New York: Oxford University Press.

----- and Werhane, P., eds. 1993. *Ethical Issues in Business: A Philosophical Approach.* 4th ed. Englewood Cliffs, New Jersey: Prentice-Hall.

----- and Dundee, T. 1994. "Toward A Unified Conception of Business Ethics: Integrative Social Contract Theory." *Academy of Management Review.* Vol. 19. Pp. 252-284.

----- 1999. *Ties That Bind: A Social Contract Approach to Business Ethics.* Cambridge, Massachusetts: Harvard Business School Press.

----- 2000. "Precis for: *Ties That Bind.*" *Business and Society Review.* Vol. 105. Pp. 436-443.

Droel, B., ed. 2000. "North American Spirituality: Cesar Chavez." *Initiatives.* No. 109. Pp. 4-5.

Dorr, R. 1928. *Susan B. Anthony: The Woman Who Changed the Mind of a Nation.* New York: Frederick A. Stokes.

Drucker, P. 1968. *The Age of Discontinuity: Guidelines to Our Changing Economy.* New York: Harper & Row.

----- 1974. *Management: Tasks, Responsibilities, Practices.* New York: Harper & Row.

Dubey, S. 1994. "After Chavez: Still Seeking Safe Sprays Out in the Fields." *Audubon.*

Vol. 96. (July-August) Pp. 22-23.

Du Bois, E., ed. 1992. *The Elizabeth Cady-Susan B. Anthony Reader: Correspondence, Writings, Speeches.* Boston: Northeastern University Press.

Dworkin, R. 1977. *Taking Rights Seriously.* Cambridge, Massachusetts: Harvard University Press.

----- 1981. "What Is Equality?" *Philosophy and Public Affairs.* Vol. 10. Pp. 185-246.

Edwards, G. 1990. *Sowing Good Seeds: The Northwest Suffrage Campaigns of SusanB. Anthony.* Portland, Oregon: Historical Society Press.

Eisler, K. 1993. *A Justice for All: William J. Brennan, Jr., and the Decisions That Transformed America.* New York: Simon & Schuster.

Ellis, J. 1986. "Religious Freedom: An American Reaction." *Vatican II Revisited.* Stackpoole, A., ed. Minneapolis: Winston. Pp. 291-297.

Federal Trade Commission Act. October, 1983. Sec. 5 (U.S. Code, 1982) USC Title 15 Sec. 4-46; Stat 717, Sec. 5.

Feinberg, J. 1980. "The Nature and Values of Rights." *Rights, Justice and Bounds of Liberty.* Princeton, New Jersey: Princeton University Press. Pp. 143-158.

Feriss, S. and Sandoval, R. 1997. *The Fight in the Fields: Cesar Chavez and the Farmworkers Movement.* New York: Harcourt Brace.

Finnis, J. 1980. *Natural Law and Natural Rights.* Oxford: Clarendon.

Fletcher, J. 1967. *Situation Ethics: The New Morality.* Philadelphia: Westminster.

Foden, D. and Morris, P., eds. 1998. *The Search for Equity.* London: Lawrence & Wishart.

Ford, J. and Kelly, G. 1959. *Contemporary Moral Theology.* Westminster, Maryland: Newman.

Frederick, R., ed. 1999. *A Companion to Business Ethics.* Malden, Massachusetts: Blackwell.

----- 1999. "An Outline of Ethical Relativism and Ethical Absolutism." *A Companion to Business Ethics.* Frederick, R., ed. Malden, Massachusetts: Blackwell. Pp.65-80.

Frederick, W. 1999. "Nature and Business Ethics." *A Companion to Business Ethics.* Frederick, R., ed. Malden, Massachusetts: Blackwell. Pp. 100-111.

Friedman, M. 1963. *Capitalism and Freedom.* Chicago: University of Chicago Press.

Gage, J. 1993. *Color and Culture: Practice and Meaning from Antiquity to Abstraction.* Boston: Little, Brown and Company.

Galbraith, J. 1952. *American Capitalism: The Concept of Countervailing Power.* Boston: Houghton Mifflin.

----- 1967. *The New Industrial State.* Boston: Houghton Mifflin.

----- 1983. *The Anatomy of Power.* Boston: Houghton Mifflin.

Gandhi, M. 1957. *An Autobiography or the Story of My Experiments with Truth* Boston: Beacon.

Gandhi, Mahatma, The Collected Works of. 1958. Delhi: Government of India.

----- 1962. *The Science of Satyagraha.* Hingorane, A., ed. Bombay: Bharatiya Videja Bhavan.

----- 1977. "The Power of Non-Violence." *The Great Documents of the World.* Heer, F., ed. New York: McGraw-Hill. Pp. 130-133.

Ganz, M. 2000. *"Resources and Resourcefulness: Strategic Capacity in the Unionization of California Agriculture, 1959-1966."* American Journal of Sociology. *Vol. 105. Pp. 103-162.*

Garcia, R. 1994. "Cesar Chavez: A Personal and Historical Testimony." *Pacific Historical Society.* Vol. 63. Pp. 51.

Garrett, T. 1966. *Business Ethics.* New York: Appleton-Century-Crofts.

----- and Klonoski, R. 1986. *Business Ethics.* 2nd ed. Englewood Cliffs, New Jersey: Prentice-Hall.

General Electric Corporation. 1968. *Our Future Business Environment: Developing Trends and Changing Institutions.* Private publication.

Gerhard, W. 1945. "The Intellectual Virtue of Prudence." *The Thomist.* Vol. 8. Pp. 413-456.

Gevisser, M. 1996. *Portraits of Power.* Capetown: David Philip.

Gewirth, A. 1983. "The Epistemology of Human Rights." *Social Philosophy and Policy.* Vol. 1. Pp. 1-24.

----- 1985. "Economic Justice: Concepts and Criteria." *Economic Justice: Private Rights and Public Responsibilities.* Kepnis, K. and Meyers, D., eds. Totowa, New Jersey: Rowan & Allaheld. Pp. 1-30.

Gioia, D. 1992. "Pinto Fires and Personal Ethics. *Journal of Business Ethics.* Vol. 11. Pp. 379-389.

Goldstein, J. 1992. *The Intelligible Constitution.* New York: Oxford University Press.

Goodpastor, K. 2001. "Conscience and its Counterfeits in Organizational Life: A New Interpretation of the Naturalist Fallacy." *Business Ethics Quarterly.* Vol. 10. Pp. 189-201.

Gordon, R. 1999. "Poisons in the Field: The United Farm Workers, Pesticides and Environmental Policies." *Pacific Historical Review.* Vol. 68, No.1. P. 51 (1).

Gould, J. 1989. "Gandhi's Relevance Today." *Gandhi's Significance for Today.* Hicks, J. and Hempel, L., eds. New York: St. Martin's Press. Pp 7-17.

Gozales, D. 1996. *Cesar Chavez: Leader for Migrant Workers.* Springfield, New York: Enslow.

Graham, S. 1996. *Woman Suffrage and the New Democracy.* New Haven, Connecticut: Yale University Press.

Guardini, R. 1961. *Power and Responsibility: A Course of Action for the New Age.* Briefs, E., trans. Chicago: Henry Regnery.

Gutierrez, G. 1973. *A Theology of Liberation.* Inda, I. and Eagleson, J., trans. Maryknoll, New York: Orbis.

Hall, E. 1976. *Beyond Culture.* Garden City, New York: Anchor Press/Doubleday.

Hagermann, A. 1996. *Nelson Mandela.* Johannesburg: Fontein.

Hamel, C. 1967. "Casuistry." *New Catholic Encyclopedia.* Washington, D.C.: Catholic University of America. Vol. 3. Pp.195-197.

Hammerback, J. and Jensen, R. 1998. *The Rhetorical Career of Cesar Chavez.* College Station: Texas A & M University Press.

Harper, J. 1998. *Susan B. Anthony: A Biographical Companion.* Santa Barbara, California: ABC-CLIO.

Havelock, E. 1978. *The Greek Concept of Justice: From the Shadows in Homer To its Substance in Plato.* Cambridge, Massachusetts: Harvard University Press.

Hebblethwaite, P. 1985. *Pope John XXIII: Shepard of the Modern World.* Garden City, New York: Doubleday.

Heer, F. 1977. "Gandhi: The Power of Non-violence." *Great Documents of the World: Milestones of Human Thought.* New York: McGraw-Hill. Pp. 130-133.

----- 1977. "The Sermon on the Mount." *Great Documents of the World: Milestones of Human Thought.* New York: McGraw-Hill. Pp. 52-55.

----- 1997. "Nicolas of Cusa: De Pace Fidei." *Great Documents of the World:*

Milestones of Human Thought. New York: McGraw-Hill. Pp. 80-83.

----- 1977. "John XXIII: Pacem in Terris.*"* *Great Documents of the World: Milestones of Human Thought.* New York: McGraw-Hill. Pp. 164-167.

Heilbroner, R. 1967. *The Worldly Philosophers.* 3rd. ed. rev. New York: Simon and Schuster.

Hempel, L. 1989. "Overview: The Elusive Legacy." *Gandhi's Significance for Today.* Hick, J. and Hempel, L., eds. New York: St. Martin's Press. Pp. 3-6.

Hick, J. 1989. "Introduction to Part I." *Gandhi's Significance for Today.* Hick, J. and Hempel, L., eds. New York: St. Martin's Press. Pp. 21-23.

Hick, J. and Hempel, L., eds. 1989. *Gandhi's Significance for Today.* New York: St. Martin's Press.

Hoffman, P. 1989. "Roncalli in the Second World War: Peace Initiatives, the Greek Famine and the Persecution of the Jews." *Journal of Ecclesiastical History.* Vol. 40. Pp. 74-99.

Holtman, S. 1998. Book Review: *Towards Justice and Virtue: A Constructive Account of Practical Reasoning.* O'Neil, O. *The Journal of Philosophy.* Vol. 95. Pp. 317-321.

Hosner, L. "Lessons from the Wreck of Exxon Valdez: The Need for Imagination, Empathy and Courage." The Ruffin Series. Special Issue #1. *Business Ethics Quarterly.* Pp. 109-122.

Hunt, J. 1989. "Gandhi in South Africa." *Gandhi's Significance for Today.* Hick, J. and Hempel, L., eds. New York: St. Martin's Press. Pp. 61-81.

Iyer, R. 1989. "Gandhi on Civilization and Religion." *Gandhi's Significance for Today.* Hick, J. and Hempel, L. New York: St. Martin's Press. Pp. 121-136.

----- 1973. *The Moral and Political Thought of Mahatma Gandhi.* Oxford University Press: New York.

Jacoby, N. 1973. *Corporate Power and Social Responsibility: A Blueprint for the Future.* New York: Macmillan.

Jaffe, A. 1964. "Symbolism in Visual Arts." *Man and His Symbols.* Jung, C., ed. Garden City, New York: Doubleday. Pp. 230-271.

James, W. 1979. *The Will to Believe.* Cambridge, Massachusetts: Harvard University Press.

John Paul II. 1981. "Laborem Exercens." *The Encyclicals of John Paul II.* Miller, I., ed. Huntington, Indiana: Our Sunday Visitor, Inc.

Johnson, F. 1969. "Civil Disobedience and the Law." *Vanderbilt Law Review.* Vol. 22. Pp.1089-1110.

Johnson, M. 1993. *Moral Imagination: Implications of Cognitive Science for Ethics.* Chicago: University of Chicago Press.

Johnston, H. 1961. *Business Ethics.* 2nd ed. rev. New York: Pitman.

John XXIII. 1963. *Pacem in Terris.* Paramus, New Jersey: Paulist.

----- 1970. *Pope John XXIII on Race and Racial Justice.* Paramus, New Jersey: Paulist.

Juerensmeyer, M. 1989. "Shoring Up the Saint: Some Suggestions for Improving Satyagraha." *Gandhi's Significance for Today.* Hick, J. and Hempel, L., eds. New York: St. Martin's Press. Pp. 36-50.

Kampe, W. 1986. "Communicating with the World: The Decree Inter Mirifica." *Vatican II Revisited.* Stackpoole, S., ed. Minneapolis: Winston.Pp. 195-201.

Kendall, F. and Louw, L. 1987. *After Apartheid: The Solution for South Africa.* San Francisco: ICS Press.

Kenealy, W. 1967. "Natural Law and Jurisprudence." *New Catholic Encyclopedia.* Washington, D.C.: Catholic University of America. Vol. 10. P. 262.

Kennedy, J. 1955. *Profiles in Courage.* New York: Harper & Brothers.

Kennedy, R. 1978. *Judge Frank Johnson, Jr.* New York: Putman.

Kepnis, K. and Meyers, D., eds. 1985. *Economic Justice: Private Rights and Public Responsibilities.* Totowa, New Jersey: Roman & Allanheld.

Khanna, S. 1985. *Gandhi and the Good Life.* New Delhi: Gandhi Peace Foundation.

Kilgore, T. 1989. "The Influence of Gandhi on Martin Luther King, Jr." *Gandhi's Significance for Today.* Hick, J. and Hempel, L., eds. New York: St. Martin's Press. Pp. 236-243.

King, M. 1964. *Why We Can't Wait.* New York: Harper and Row.

Kinsella, J. 1967. "Boycott." *New Catholic Encyclopedia.* Washington, D.C.: Catholic University of America. Vol. 2. Pp.741-742.

Kolm, S-C. 1996. *Modern Theories of Justice.* Cambridge, Massachusetts: MIT Press.

Konig, F. 1986. "The Right to Religious Freedom: The Significance of Dignitatis Humanae. Stackpoole, A., ed. *Vatican II Revisited.* Minneapolis: Winston. Pp. 283-290.

Kotter, J. 1977. "Power, Dependence, and Effective Management." *Harvard Business*

Review. Vol. 55. July-August. Pp. 125-136.

Kung, H. 1986. "Catholics and Protestants: An Ecumenical Inventory." Stackpoole, A., ed. *Vatican II Revisited.* Minneapolis: Winston. Pp. 24-31.

La Forge, P. 2000. "Four Steps to a Fundamental Ethical Vision through Meditation." *Journal of Business Ethics.* Vol. 28. Pp. 25-34.

Larmore, C. 1981. "Moral Judgment." *Review of Metaphysics.* Vol. 35. Pp. 275-296.

Levy, J. 1975. *Cesar Chavez: Autobiography of La Causa.* New York: Norton.

Lineberry, W., ed. 1972. *Justice in America: Law, Order, and the Courts.* New York: H. W. Wilson.

Lucas, S. 1971. "Against Equality." *Justice and Equality.* Brody, B., ed. Englewood Cliffs, New Jersey: Prentice-Hall. Pp. 138-151.

Lukes, S. 1992. "Power." *Encyclopedia of Ethics.* Becker, L., ed. Vol. 925. New York: Garlandling. P. 995.

Luthans, F. and Hodgetts, eds. 1972. *Readings in the Current Social Issues in Business: Poverty, Civil Rights, Ecology and Consumerism.* New York: Macmillan.

Machiavelli, N. 1998. *The Prince.* Bull, G., trans. Harmondworth: Penguin.

MacIntyre, A. 1981. *After Virtue.* Notre Dame, Indiana: University of Notre Dame Press.

----- 1988. *Whose Justice? Which Rationality?* Notre Dame, Indiana: University of Notre Dame Press.

Maitland, I. 2001. "Distributive Justice in Firms: Do the Rules of Corporate Governance Matter?" *Business Ethics Quarterly.* Vol. 11. Pp. 129-144.

Mandela, N. 1994. *Long Walk to Freedom: The Autobiography of Nelson Mandela.* Boston: Little, Brown and Company.

----- 1996. *Mandela: An Illustrated Autobiography.* Boston: Little, Brown.

Marilley, S. 1996. *Woman Suffrage and the Origins of Liberal Feminism In the United States, 1820-1920.* Cambridge, Massachusetts: Harvard University Press.

Maritain, J. 1948. *The Person and the Common Good.* London: Geoffrey Bles.

----- 1951. *Man and the State.* Chicago: University of Chicago Press.

----- 1964. *Moral Philosophy: An Historical and Critical Survey of the Great Systems.* New York: Charles Scribner's Sons.

Maund, B. 1995. *Colours: Their Nature and Representation.* New York: Cambridge

University Press.

McBrien, R. 1980. *Catholicism.* Minneapolis: Winston.

McCollough, T. 1991. *The Moral Imagination and the Public Life.* Chatham, New Jersey: Chatham House.

McCormick, R. and Ramsey, P., eds. 1978. *Doing Evil to Achieve Good: Moral Choices in Conflict Situations.* Chicago: Loyola University Press.

McCurry, J. 1997. "Loyalty Saves Malden Mills." *Textile World.* Vol. 147. N. 2. Pp. 38-45.

----- 1997. "TW's 1997 Leader of the Year: Aaron Feuerstein." *Textile World.* Vol. 147. N. 10. Pp. 34-40.

McDonagh, E., ed. 1965. *Moral Theology Renewed.* Dublin: Gill and Son.

McGlynn, J. and Toner, J. 1967. *Modern Ethical Theories.* Milwaukee: Bruce.

McGovern, A. 1981. "Marxism and Christianity." *New Catholic Encyclopedia.* Washington, D.C.: Catholic University of America. Vol. 17. Pp. 391.

McGrath, M. 1986. "Social Teaching Since the Council: A Response from Latin Americana." *Vatican II Revisited.* Stackpoole, A., ed. Minneapolis: Winston. Pp. 324-336.

McKinley, D. 1997. *The ANC and the Liberation Struggle: A Political Biography.* London: Pluto.

McMahon, T. 1973. "The Moral Aspects of Power." *Power and the Word of God.* Bockle, F. and Pohier, J-M., eds. New York: Herder and Herder. Pp. 51-65.

----- 1997. "History of Business Ethics." *The Blackwell Encyclopedic Dictionary of Business Ethics.* Werhane, P. and Freeman. R., eds. Malden, Massachusetts: Blackwell. Pp. 317-320.

----- 1997. "Transforming Justice." *The Blackwell Encyclopedic Dictionary of Business Ethics.* Werhane, P. and Freeman, R., eds. Malden, Massachusetts: Blackwell. Pp. 630-632.

----- 1999. "From Social Irresponsibility to Social Responsiveness: The Chrysler/Kenosha Plant Closing." *Journal of Business Ethics.* Vol. 20. Pp. 101-111.

----- 1999. "Transforming Justice: A Conceptualization." *Business Ethics Quarterly.* Vol. 9. Pp. 593-602.

----- 2000. "Lifeboat Ethics in Business." *Business Ethics Quarterly.* Vol. 10. Pp. 269-276.

McPartlan. 2001. "The Legacy of Vatican II in the Pontificate of John Paul II." *New New Catholic Encyclopedia.* Washington, D.C.: Gale Group/The Catholic University of America

Meredith, M. *Nelson Mandela: A Biography.* London: Hamish Hamilton.

Messner, J. 1949. *Social Ethics.* St.Louis: B. Herder.

Miller, D. 1976. *Social Justice.* Oxford: Oxford University Press.

Miller, J., ed. 1966. *Vatican II: An Interfaith Appraisal.* Notre Dame, Indiana: University of Notre Dame Press.

Mills, N. 1993. "Remembering Cesar Chavez." *Dissent.* Vol. 40. Pp. 552-553.

Mitchell, C. 1997. "The Old Man: A Nation's Revered Spirit." *World Business.* Vol. 3. P. 24.

Moberg, D. Book Review: *Moral Imagination and Management Decision Making.* Werhane, P. *Business Ethics Quarterly.* Vol. 11. Pp. 373-377.

Montague, A. 1969. *Man: His First Two Million Years.* New York: Columbia University Press.

Moorman, J. 1986. "Observers and Guests of the Council." *Vatican II Revisited.* Stackpoole, A., ed. Minneapolis: Winston. Pp. 155-169.

Morgan, C. 1979. *One Man, One Voice.* New York: Holt, Rinehart and Winston.

Mundschenk, P. "The Heart of Satyagraha: A Quest for Inner Dignity, Not Political Power." *Gandhi's Significance for Today.* Hick, J. and Hempel, L., eds. New York: St. Martin's Press. Pp. 24-35.

Murthy, B., ed. 1987. *Mahatma Gandhi and Leo Tolstoy Letters.* Long Beach, California: Long Beach Publications.

Nahser, B. 1997. *Learning to Read the Signs: Reclaiming Pragmatism in Business.* Boston: Butterworth-Heinemann.

----- and Ruhe, J. 2001. "Putting American Pragmatism to Work in the Classroom. *Journal of Business Ethics.* Vol. 24. Pp. 317-330.

National Council of Catholic Bishops. 1986. *Economic Justice for All.* Washington, D.C.: U.S. Catholic Conference.

Noonan, J. 1984. *Bribes.* Berkeley: University of California Press.

Nossiter, B. 1964. *The Mythmakers: An Essay on Power and Wealth.* Boston: Houghton Mifflin.

Nozick, R. 1974. *Anarchy, State and Utopia.* New York: Basic Books.

Nuesse, C. 1967. "Discrimination." *New Catholic Encyclopedia.* Washington, D.C.: Catholic University of America. Vol. 4. Pp. 897.

O'Callaghan, D. 1965. "The Meaning of Justice." *Moral Theology Renewed.* McDonagh, E., ed. Dublin: Gill and Son. Pp. 151-172.

O'Donohoe. J. 1967. "Sin (Theology)." *New Catholic Encyclopedia* Washington, D.C.: Catholic University of America. Vol. 17. Pp. 610-611.

O'Neil, O. 1996. *Towards Justice and Virtue: A Constructive Account of Practical Reasoning.* New York: Cambridge University Press.

Ostergaard,G. 1989. "The Gandhian Movement in India Since the Death of Gandhi." *Gandhi's Significance for Today.* Hick, J. and Hempel, L., eds. New York: St. Martin's Press. Pp. 203-225.

Ottaway, D. 1993. *Chained Together: Mandela, de Klerk and the Struggle to Remake South Africa.* New York: Times Books.

Outler, A. 1986. "Strangers Within the Gates." *Vatican II Revisited.* Stackpoole, A., ed. Minneapolis: Winston. Pp. 170-183.

Oyewole, P. 2000. "Social Costs of Environmental Justice Associated with the Practice of Green Marketing." *Journal of Business Ethics.* Vol. 29. Pp. 239-251.

Ozar, D. 1986. "Rights: What They Are and Where They Come From." *Philosophical Issues in Human Rights: Theories and Applications.* Werhane, P., Gini, A. and Ozar, D., eds. New York: Random House. Pp. 3-25.

Parry, R. 1996. *Plato's Craft of Justice.* Albany: State University of New York Press.

Philip, D. 1994. *Nelson Mandela Speaks: Forging a Democracy.* Johannesburg: Nonracial South Africa.

Pieper, J. 1965. *The Four Cardinal Virtues: Prudence, Justice. Fortitude, Temperance.* New York: Harcourt, Brace & World.

Perreault, W., and McCarthy, E. 1986. *Basic Marketing: A Global Managerial Approach.* 12 ed. Chicago: Richard D. Irwin.

Plato. 1957. *The Republic.* Landsay, A., trans. New York: Dutton.

Plessy v. Ferguson. 163. U.S. 537 (1896).

Post, J. 2002. "The 'Iron Law' of Business Responsibility Revisited: Lessons from South Africa." Book Review: *Economic Imperatives and Ethical Values in Global Business: The South African Experience and International Codes Today.* Seth, S. and Williams, O. *Business Ethics Quarterly.* Vol. 12. Pp.

265-276.

Purcell, T. and Cavanagh, G. 1972. *Blacks in the Industrial World: Issues for the Managers.* New York: Free Press.

Railton, P. 1986. "Moral Realism." *Philosophical Review.* Vol. 95. Pp. 163-207.

Ramsey, P. 1962. *Nine Modern Moralists.* Englewood Cliffs, New Jersey: Prentice-Hall.

Rawls, J. 1971. *A Theory of Justice.* Cambridge, Massachusetts: Harvard University Press.

----- 1971. "Justice as Fairness." *Justice and Equality.* Brody, B. Engelwood Cliffs, New Jersey: Prentice-Hall. Pp. 76-102.

Rayhavan, I. 1973. *The Moral and Political Thought of Mahatma Gandhi.* Delhi: Oxford University Press.

Rees, J. 1972. *Equality.* London: Macmillan.

Regan, D. and DeVeer, V., eds. 1982. *And Justice for All.* Totowa, New Jersey: Roman & Allanheld.

Richards, D. 1982. "Justice and Equality." *And Justice for All.* Regan, T. and VanDeVeer, D, eds. Totowa, New Jersey: Rowman & Allanheld. Pp. 241-263.

Rozak, J. 1969. *The Making of A Counter Culture.* New York: Anchor-Doubleday.

Rosales, R. 1996. *Chicano? The History of the Mexican-American Civil Rights.* Houston: Arte Publico Press.

Rowan, J. 2001. Book Review: *Ties That Bind: A Social Contract Approach to Business Ethics* . Donaldson, T. and Dundee, T. *Business Ethics Quarterly.* Vol. 11. Pp. 379-390.

Royidis, E. 1961. *Pope John.* New York: Viking.

Ryan, J. 2001. "Moral Reasoning as a Determinate of Organizational Citizenship Behaviors: A Study in the Public Accounting Profession." *Journal of Business Ethics.* Vol. 33. Pp. 233-244.

Sampson, A. 1999. *Mandela: The Authorized Biography.* New York: Alfred A. Knopf.

Schnitzer, M. 1990. *Contemporary Government and Business Relations.* 4th ed. Boston: Houghton Mifflin.

Schussler-Fiorenza, F. 1981. "Liberation Theology." *New Catholic Encyclopedia.*

Washington, D.C.: Catholic University of America. Vol. 17. P. 350.

Scab, P., ed. 1977. *Great Documents of the World: Milestones of Human Thought.* New York: McGraw-Hill.

Seeder, M. and Ulcer, R. 2001. "Virtuous Responses to Organizational Crisis: Aaron Feuerstein and Milt Cole." *Journal of Business Ethics.* Vol. 31. Pp. 369-376.

Selekman, S. and B. 1956. *Power and Morality in a Business Society.* New York: McGraw.

Selznick, P. 1957. *Leadership in Administration.* New York: Harper & Row.

Sethi, S. and Williams, O. 2000. *Economic Imperatives and Ethical Values in Global Business: The South African Experience and International Codes Today.* Boston: Kluwer Academic Publishers. Reprint: 2001. Notre Dame, Indiana: The University of Notre Dame Press.

Shaw, B. 1999. "Aristotle and Posner on Corrective Justice: The Tortoise and the Hare." *Business Ethics Quarterly.* Vol. 9. Pp. 651-657.

Sherr, L. 1995. *Failure Is Impossible: Susan B. Anthony In Her Own Words.* New York: Times Books.

Shostram, E. 1967. *Man the Manipulator.* Nashville: Abingdon.

Sikorski, R. 1996. "How We Lost Poland: Heroes Do Not Make Politicians." *Foreign Affairs.* Vol. 75. Pp. 15-22.

Skinner, B. 1972. *Beyond Freedom and Dignity.* New York: Alfred A. Knopf.

Smith, S. 1989. "Gandhi's Moral Philosophy." *Gandhi's Significance for Today.* Hicks, J. and Hempel, L. New York: St. Martin's Press. Pp. 109-121.

Solomon, R. and Murphy, M., eds. 1990. *What is Justice: Classic and Contemporary Readings.* New York: Oxford University Press.

Spleft, J. 1970. "Symbol." *Sacramentum Mundi.* New York: Herder and Herder. Vol. 6. Pp. 199-203.

Sterba, J. 1994. "Reconciling Conceptions of Justice." *Morality and Social Justice.* Sterba, J. et al. Lanham, Maryland: Rowman and Littlefield. Pp. 1-38.

----- 1998. *Justice for Here and Now.* New York: Cambridge University Press.

Stevenson, J. 1971. *The Montgomery Bus Boycott.* New York: Franklin Watts.

Stone, J. 1965. *Human Law and Human Justice.* London: Stevens and Sons Limited.

Stransky, T. 1986. "The Foundation of the Secretariat for Promoting Christian Unity."

Vatican II Revisited. Stackpoole, A., ed. Minneapolis: Winston. Pp. 62-87.

Suenens, L-J. 1986. "A Plan for the Whole Council." *Vatican II Revisited.* Stackpoole, A., ed. Minneapolis: Winston. Pp. 88-105.

Sumner, L. 1987. *The Moral Foundation of Rights.* Oxford: Clarendon.

Sun OS, B. 1999. "Relying on Faith to Rebuild A Business." *Workforce.* Vol. 78. No. 3. Pp. 54-59.

Supreme Court of the United States. October Term. 1964. No. 37. *Textiles Workers of America, Petitioner, v. Darlington Manufacturing Company et al.; National Labor Relations Board, Petitioners v. Darlington Manufacturing Company et al. NLRB Case No. 11-CA-1075.*

Sutton, F., Harris, S., Caisson, C. and Tobin, J. 1956. *The American Business Creed.* Cambridge, Massachusetts: Harvard University Press.

Synod of Bishops. 1992. "Justice in the World." *Catholic Social Thought: The Documentary Heritage.* O'Brien, D. and Shannon, T., eds. Mary knoll, New York: Obis.

Tawny, R. 1964. *Equality.* 4th ed. London: Unpin.

Taylor, R. 1975. *Chavez and the Farm Workers.* Boston: Beacon.

Teal, T. 1996. "Not a Fool, Not a Saint." *Fortune.* (November 11.) Pp. 201-204.

Thomson, J. 1990. *The Realm of Rights.* Cambridge, Massachusetts: Harvard University Press.
Taillike, P. 1954. *Love, Power, and Justice.* New York: Oxford University Press.

Frisco, R. 1967. "John XXIII, Pope." *New Catholic Encyclopedia.* Washington, D.C.: Catholic University of America. Vol. 7. Pp. 1015-1020.

----- 1967. "Vatican Council II." *New Catholic Encyclopedia.* Washington, D.C.: Catholic University of America. Vol. 14. Pp. 563-72.

Tuck, R. 1979. Natural Rights Theories: Their Origin and Development. Cambridge: Cambridge University Press.

Turner, J. and Valentine, S. 2001. "Cynicism as a Fundamental Dimension of Moral Decision-Making." *Journal of Business Ethics.* Vol. 34. Pp. 123-136.

Tutu, D. 1984. *Crying in the Wilderness.* Grand Rapids, Michigan: William B. Eerdmones.

----- 1994. *The Rainbow People of God.* Allen, J., ed. London: Doubleday.

United Nations Department of Public Information. 1994. *The United Nations and*

Apartheid 1948-1994. New York.

Urofsky, M. 1991. *A Conflict of Rights: The Supreme Court and Affirmative Action.* New York: Scribner's.

Vatican Council II. 1966. "Pastoral Constitution on the Church in the Modern World." *The Documents of Vatican II.* Abbot, W., ed. New York: Guild. Pp. 199-308, #5.

Vines, K. 1964. "Federal Judges and Race Relations in the South." *Journal of Politics.* Vol. 2. Pp. 337-357.

Von Buren, H. 2001. "If Fairness Is the Problem, Is Consent the Solution? Integrating ISCT and Stakeholder Theory." *Business Ethics Quarterly.* Vol. 11. Pp. 481-500.

Vorgrimler, H. 1986. "Karl Rahner: The Theologian's Contribution." *Vatican II Revisited.* Stackpoole, A., ed. Minneapolis: Winston. Pp. 32-46.

Walton, C. 1969. *Ethos and the Executive.* Englewood Cliffs, New Jersey: Prentice-Hall.

Walker, M. 1983. *Spheres of Justice: A Defense of Pluralism and Equality.* Oxford: Blackwell.

----- 1994. *Thick and Thin.* Notre Dame, Indiana: Notre Dame University Press.

Weinreb. L. 1987. *Natural Law and Justice.* Cambridge, Massachusetts: Harvard University Press.

Wekesser C. and Swisher, K., eds. 1990. *Social Justice: Opposing Viewpoints.* San Diego, California: Gruhaven.

Werhane, P. 1985. *Persons, Rights and Corporations.* Englewood Cliffs, New Jersey: Prentice-Hall.

----- 1998. "Moral Imagination and the Search for Ethical Decision Making in Management." The Ruffin Series, Special Issue #1. *Business Ethics Quarterly.* Pp.75-98.

----- 1999. *Moral Imagination and Management Decision Making.* New York: Oxford University Press.

Westphal, J. 1991. *Colour: A Philosophical Introduction.* Oxford: Blackwell.

Whetstone, J. 2001. "How Virtue Fits Within Business Ethics." *Journal of Business Ethics.* Vol. 30. Pp. 101-114.

Willebrands, J. 1986. "Christians and Jews: A New Vision." *Vatican II Revisited.* Stackpoole, A., ed. Minneapolis: Winston. Pp. 220-236.

Williams, B.   1971.   "The Idea of Equality."   *Justice and Equality.*   Brody, B., ed.
Englewood Cliffs, New Jersey: Prentice-Hall. Pp. 116-137.

Wu, J. 1967. "Natural Law." *New Catholic Encyclopedia.* Washington, D.C.: Catholic
University of America. Vol. 10. P. 256.

Zahn, G. 1971. "The Great Catholic Upheaval." *SR.* (September 11.) Pp. 24-56.

About the Author

Thomas F. McMahon, C.S.V. is Professor Emeritus in the School of Business Administration of Loyola University Chicago. He had taught Business Ethics at in the Graduate School of Business for 28 years, where he was also the Director of the Center for Values in Business. Fr. McMahon is an ordained Roman Catholic priest who received his doctorate in Theology from the University of St. Thomas Aquinas (known as the Angelicum) in Rome, Italy and an M.B.A. degree from George Washington University. He has authored more than 60 articles related to business ethics and has given hundreds of presentations on related topics. His work on Transforming Justice is an original conceptualization that has appeared in *Business Ethics Quarterly* and *The Dictionary of Business Ethics*.

INDEX